COUNCIL *on*
FOREIGN
RELATIONS

Council Special Report No. 90
February 2021

The United States, China, and Taiwan: A Strategy to Prevent War

Robert D. Blackwill and Philip Zelikow

CONTENTS

FOREWORD

It is something of a cliché, but no less true for being so, to note that the relationship between the United States and China will go a long way toward determining the character of this century. The challenge for the two countries will be to pursue their often diverging interests and goals in a manner that does not lead to direct confrontation and that keeps open the possibility of cooperation on those occasions in which their interests happen to overlap. Accomplishing this—successfully managing a growing rivalry—will surely strain the diplomatic skills of both governments.

Taiwan is the issue with the greatest potential to turn competition into direct confrontation. For the past four decades, diplomatic finesse, backed by military deterrence, has maintained a precarious peace in the Taiwan Strait. The United States has played a critical role in deterring China from using force against Taiwan, as Beijing cannot be sure that the United States would stand aside in the face of Chinese aggression. Similarly, the United States has deterred Taiwan from seeking formal independence, as Taipei cannot be certain that the United States would come to its defense should it provoke a Chinese assault.

Cross-strait stability has allowed Taiwan to thrive and its people to build a democratic, pluralistic, and economically vibrant society. China, for its part, benefited from Taiwanese investment on the mainland and was able to set military modernization aside for a time to focus instead on economic development. The United States, through its One China policy, maintained official diplomatic relations with China but at the same time built a strong unofficial relationship with Taiwan.

It is unclear, however, whether this playbook that has worked so well for forty years can endure. Xi Jinping has broken from his predecessors, who stressed maintaining a low profile internationally and were content with keeping the question of Taiwan unresolved in order to focus on economic growth, recognizing that a Taiwan crisis would seriously harm China's economy. Xi has opted for a more assertive Chinese foreign policy. On his watch, China has militarized the South China Sea, fought border skirmishes with India, challenged Japanese claims to the Senkaku islands, and used economic leverage to punish countries critical of Chinese practices. Xi has also overseen an effort to intimidate Taiwan and signaled that the Taiwan question cannot be delayed indefinitely.

China now possesses a stronger military that it hopes to rely on to back this bolder foreign policy. China has the second-largest military budget in the world, and most of its focus has gone toward preparing for a Taiwan scenario. In the United States, there has been a push toward retrenchment, while the Donald J. Trump administration called into question the value of America's alliances and partnerships. As a result, China has greater capabilities to coerce Taiwan, and it could very well be questioning whether the United States would intervene on Taiwan's behalf despite the fact that the Joe Biden administration has signaled that it well might. The net result is that the chances of a conflict over Taiwan have grown significantly in recent years.

It is in this context that Robert D. Blackwill, the Henry A. Kissinger senior fellow for U.S. foreign policy at the Council on Foreign Relations, and Philip Zelikow, the White Burkett Miller professor of history and Wilson Newman professor of governance at the University of Virginia, have written this Council Special Report, which aims to put forward a strategy to prevent a conflict in the Taiwan Strait. Blackwill and Zelikow argue that U.S. strategy is inadequate to deter or if need be react to Chinese coercion or aggression. The authors suggest how this gap could be narrowed. They also recommend (prudently, I believe) that the United States maintain its One China policy, closely coordinate U.S.-Taiwan policy with Japan and other Asian allies, support Taiwan's position in international organizations that do not require statehood for membership, conclude a bilateral trade agreement with Taiwan, and build people-to-people ties with Taiwan.

Some will argue that the report's recommendations do not go far enough in calling for adjusting upwards either the means (in my case, for example, choosing strategic clarity over ambiguity when it comes to U.S. readiness to come to Taiwan's defense if China triggers a crisis) or even the ends of U.S. policy (i.e., calling for the United States to recognize Taiwan's independence). Some will argue the opposite, that the authors go too far and risk getting the United States embroiled in a conflict that is not vital to U.S. interests. Such a range of reactions is to be expected, even welcomed.

What cannot be disputed is that the stakes are enormous and that what happens in the Taiwan Strait will have ramifications for the future of Asia, America's alliance system and presence in the region, and the U.S.-China relationship. As a result, the authors have done a true service in providing rigorous thinking to help guide the Biden administration, Congress, and the public as they consider U.S. policy on this critical issue.

Richard N. Haass
President
Council on Foreign Relations
February 2021

ACKNOWLEDGMENTS

We commend the 109 members of the Council on Foreign Relations (CFR) Study Group on U.S. policy toward Taiwan for their insights during our eight sessions over the past four months and are grateful for Gary Roughead's co-chairmanship of the meetings. We appreciate Raymond F. Burghardt, Evan A. Feigenbaum, Michael J. Green, Patricia M. Kim, Evan Medeiros, Randall G. Schriver, and Susan A. Thornton for presenting their findings to the group and for comments on our draft report from Roughead, Burghardt, Feigenbaum, and Kim, as well as those from Graham Allison, Elizabeth Economy, and Robert Zoellick. We thank CFR President Richard N. Haass for his review and incisive comments, Patricia Dorff and the CFR Publications team for their editorial contributions, and Daniel Clay for his extensive research.

The analysis and conclusions are the authors' responsibility alone.

Robert D. Blackwill and Philip Zelikow

"Great is the guilt of an unnecessary war."

—John Adams

A GATHERING STORM

We wrote this report because, during 2020, we came to believe that a crisis was building over Taiwan and that it was becoming the most dangerous flash point in the world for a possible war that involved the United States of America, China, and probably other major powers. We think this danger is half understood intellectually, but it is downplayed in the invariable human tendency to assume that whatever the commotion, tomorrow will be pretty much like yesterday. This is an old problem. With the two exceptions of the German invasion of Poland in 1939 and the American and British invasion of Iraq in 2003, the outbreak of practically every international war since 1900 has come as a surprise, except to those who were planning the war.

What even many watchers of world politics could neglect, distracted by so many other global problems and noisemakers, is how much the situation surrounding Taiwan has changed in the last few years. As we will detail, China's decision to crush local governance and effective rule of law in Hong Kong has had large effects. It changed politics in Taiwan in favor of the reelection of its serving president. Chinese leaders doubled down on xenophobic nationalism and repression, escalating pressure on Taiwan both rhetorically and militarily. Taiwan has begun a significant program of rearmament with a seriousness not seen in a generation, supported by the United States, yet there is a significant window of time before this program can bear much fruit.

Later in this report we recall the example of the great war crisis over Czechoslovakia in the autumn of 1938. That crisis too was set off by the rippling effects of changing circumstances, in that case the aftermath of the German annexation of Austria in March 1938 and the tense demands that followed later that spring that, on the surface, were about how to define the limits and character of Germany. Of course, differences between that case and this one are numerous. Our point is to stress how dynamic the circumstances can be and how quickly seemingly remote tests of resolve can arise.

By June 2020, a sober and experienced observer, James Stavridis, retired admiral and former North Atlantic Treaty Organization (NATO) supreme commander, commented that "there is a cogent argument to be made at the most senior levels in Beijing that this is a perfect moment for a strike on Taiwan. But I would ascribe less than a 1 in 4 chance that they make a military move in the immediate future, i.e., before US elections [in November 2020]."[1] We think Admiral Stavridis had that about right. To that assessment, which no prudent person would find comforting, we add that we believe 2021 is already shaping up as more dangerous than 2020.

That is the context in which we examined apparent U.S. strategy for such a conflict and found it wanting. We do not believe such U.S. strategy as it exists is adequately coordinated with, at a minimum, Taiwan and Japan. We do not think it is politically or militarily realistic to count on a U.S. military defeat of various kinds of Chinese assaults on Taiwan, uncoordinated with allies. Nor is it realistic to presume that, after such a frustrating clash, the United States would or should simply escalate to some sort of wide-scale war against China with comprehensive blockades or strikes against targets on the Chinese mainland.

If U.S. campaign plans postulate such unrealistic scenarios, they will likely be rejected by an American president and the U.S. Congress (if the Congress gets to decide, reflecting the interests of the American people). The resulting U.S. paralysis would not be the result of presidential weakness or timidity. It could arise because the most powerful country in the world did not have credible options prepared for the most dangerous military crisis looming in front of it.

We believe that credible options for a Taiwan crisis can be readied, ones the president could meaningfully consider. They could seek to avoid a confrontation and strengthen deterrence. They could rest on Taiwan's will and readiness to defend its democracy. They could rest on Japan's readiness, with the United States, to help Taiwan defend itself.

At the beginning of 2021, the Donald J. Trump administration's leaders left behind an increasingly dangerous case. Watching a fire approach, ignited by the People's Republic of China's (PRC) behavior and Taiwan's reactions, they sprayed gasoline toward it, having only a garden hose nearby. It is not much of an answer to say that advanced firefighting equipment could be ordered and could arrive in a few years, even as the fire grows.

Our answer is, first, stop spraying gasoline. Second, immediately develop a more credible firefighting strategy, one that does not rely either on the garden hose or on the imagined equipment that could arrive years from now.

On January 23, reacting to Chinese moves, the new Joe Biden administration issued a prepared statement entitled "PRC Military Pressure Against Taiwan Threatens Regional Peace and Stability." The statement urged Beijing to "cease its military, diplomatic, and economic pressure against Taiwan and instead engage in meaningful dialogue with Taiwan's democratically elected representatives." While soothingly reaffirming the historic U.S. postures on Taiwan that we describe later in this report, the Biden administration added that it would keep "deepening our ties with democratic Taiwan" and it then said, perhaps fatefully, "Our commitment to Taiwan is rock-solid and contributes to the maintenance of peace and stability across the Taiwan Strait and within the region." The tone of this statement is "rock-solid." Yet the underlying substance of "our commitment" is no clearer than it was before.

In this report, we propose a realistic strategic objective for Taiwan, and the associated policy prescriptions, to sustain the political balance that has kept the peace for the last fifty years. We pair that with a strategy that relies less on U.S. aircraft carriers sailing to the rescue in waters their enemy dominates and more on coordinated planning to help Taiwan defend itself.

The United States, Japan, and perhaps others could rapidly prepare a coordinated allied military challenge to various kinds of assaults on Taiwan to help the Taiwanese defend themselves in an emergency and to force China to make a choice about whether it wants a wider, if still limited, war. If Beijing chooses such a war, the United States, Japan, and other allies could seek to keep the war limited, militarily, while preparing—visibly, in advance—all the disruptive political, economic, and military mobilization measures that would likely follow the outbreak of such a conflict.

The place to begin to assess options regarding U.S. policy toward Taiwan is to judge how important Taiwan is to U.S. national interests; it is striking that many pundits ignore this preeminent factor in their analyses. Putting aside the frequent instinct by regional experts to consider nearly every inch of Mother Earth as vital to the United States, we believe that only a few pieces of real estate anywhere are in that category. Strictly defined as necessary to safeguard and enhance Americans' survival in a free and secure nation, a traditional definition of vital U.S. national interests is that they are to

1. prevent the use and reduce the threat of nuclear, biological, and chemical weapons and catastrophic conventional terrorist attacks or cyber-attacks against the United States, its military forces abroad, or its allies;

2. stop the spread of nuclear weapons, secure nuclear weapons and materials, and reduce further proliferation of intermediate- and long-range delivery systems for nuclear weapons;

3. maintain a global and regional balance of power that promotes peace, stability, and freedom through domestic U.S. robustness, U.S. international power projection and influence, and the strength of U.S. alliance systems;

4. prevent the emergence of hostile major powers or failed states on U.S. borders; and

5. ensure the viability and stability of major global systems (trade, financial markets, public health, energy supplies, cyberspace, the environment, and freedom of the seas).[2]

During the last generation, the fifth point—threats to global systems—has become more salient, brought home throughout the world by the current pandemic, the accelerating changes in global climate, and the recent international financial crisis.

Taiwan obviously does not qualify directly in any of these vital U.S. national interests—contrasted with Europe, Canada and Mexico, and members of the United States' Asian alliances. Taiwan does not possess catastrophic weapons and it is not attempting to acquire them.[3] It has no influence on whether such weapons and their missile delivery systems proliferate. Far from North America, it also will have no influence on the viability of major global systems. Even if China used Taiwan as a military forward operating base, it would not threaten "Americans' survival in a free and secure nation."

We are left with U.S. vital national interest number three, the relationship of the future of Taiwan to peace, stability, and freedom in East Asia. The U.S. government is not obligated by treaty to help defend Taiwan from attack but it is required by the Taiwan Relations Act to help Taiwan defend itself.

In considering the significance of Taiwan, it does matter that this is no longer the retreating remnant of a dictatorial Kuomintang regime, licking its wounds from defeat in a Chinese civil war. That was a long time ago. Taiwan is now *the* large example of a Chinese-speaking democracy and has its own emerging sense of identity.[4]

We live at a time in world history in which the relative appeal of a supposed China model of technocratic totalitarianism will have a large, intangible influence on choices that many societies are making, in Asia and beyond. The relatively recent rise of a truly democratic Taiwan chafes China in a way that the existence of lively West Berlin, sitting in the middle of the communist German Democratic Republic, stood as a sort of existential challenge to that state, and to its communist allies in Europe (and the Soviet bloc). Hong Kong had some of this quality too, which became intolerable to leaders in Beijing.

Were China to use military might to rub out the Taiwan irritant, it would implicate issues about the world's future that go beyond Taiwan and its tens of millions of inhabitants. Or, perhaps, some could argue that if China extinguished its Taiwan problem, it would become satisfied and secure. Neighbors like Japan would naturally react, however, with understandable alarm. If China found those reactions menacing, then new issues could arise, perhaps starting with the nearby Ryukyu Islands.

Also, if the United States did not meaningfully respond to PRC military action against Taiwan with U.S. use of force and allowed Taiwan to be conquered by China, would U.S. treaty allies Japan and South Korea, not to say the Baltic states, already racked with doubt because of the Trump presidency, conclude that Washington could not be counted on to defend them?[5] In the context of vital national interest number three, could the United States in that situation maintain "the strength of U.S. alliance systems," or would Japan in particular reason that it could only ensure its sovereignty and freedom in the face of Chinese power by acquiring nuclear weapons, a feat Japan could probably accomplish in less than a year?[6]

This argument has a quality of domino theory, showing all the weaknesses displayed half a century ago in regard to Vietnam, and it is far from certain that the Taiwan dominoes would fall in this disastrous way. But that does not make this domino scenario any less compelling for many today. However, as with all domino theories, there is no way to know in advance if worst-case projections would actually occur.[7] An open-ended and ill-defined commitment to go to war with China driven by an unverifiable theory would test the character and judgment of any American president.

Any student of the history of U.S. national security decision-making recognizes that many factors can go into such presidential decisions. These include the president's experience, character, and domestic priorities; the health or otherwise of the U.S. economy and society; the president's perspective on U.S. vital national interests; the strength of the U.S. international position; the circumstances that led up to the crisis; whether the president believes in domino theories; the views of his principal advisors; the quality of analyses, staff work, and intelligence within the administration; major attitudes in the Congress; U.S. public opinion; the views of allies; and the capabilities and skills of the enemy.

With all these factors in mind, it is impossible to know before the crisis whether the United States would use military force to defend Taiwan against a Chinese attack, or even whether it should. That would also depend on the vigor and resilience of the Taiwanese people and on the attitudes of crucial neighbors, especially Japan. Our impression is that Japanese opinion about a possible Chinese assault on Taiwan would be strong, but that it is also inchoate, divided, volatile, and untested. Japan's leaders have not yet chosen to guide it in a determined way. Yet, amid all these uncertainties, what the U.S. government can do now, working with its friends, before the crisis, is to prepare more credible, visible plans for how it and they could respond.

The U.S. strategic objective regarding Taiwan should be to preserve its political and economic autonomy, its dynamism as a free society, and U.S.-allied deterrence—without triggering a Chinese attack on Taiwan. To the uninitiated, this may seem a straightforward and mechanical process. It is not. It would depend on Washington's accurate and enduring estimate of China's sufferance for such U.S. policies toward Taiwan, and the strength of Beijing's commitment to its existing and perhaps future red lines.

Regarding its tolerance for Washington's rhetoric and actions concerning Taiwan, China is far from transparent. Thus Washington could inadvertently misread the public and private statements from Beijing, not to say the pressures within the Chinese leadership and PRC domestic events, which could trigger aggressive PRC behavior regarding Taiwan. In respect to China's current red lines, we deduce that they are: no declaration of independence by Taiwan and "no external interference," which we interpret to mean no U.S. troop deployments in Taiwan and no security pact between the United States and Taiwan.

In any case, implementing our proposed strategic objective would require quality U.S. decision-making and policies. Successful diplomacy is to a large degree situational and takes place under changing circumstances, which requires tactical adjustments; it does not resemble a cookbook recipe. Given the potentially catastrophic consequences of misjudgment, the Biden administration's continuing order of the day regarding policy toward Taiwan should be prudent caution, but not timidity.

We would like to be wrong about the possible seriousness of a coming Taiwan crisis. We hope we have exaggerated the danger. We just cannot persuade ourselves that the ominous clouds we see gathering are not really there.

U.S.-CHINA RELATIONS DETERIORATE

U.S.-China relations are bad, at a historic low point in the past half century, and are unlikely to fundamentally improve under President Biden's administration.[8] With that ominous premise, we advance seven macro principles that provide the strategic context and guide our analysis regarding the future of U.S. policy toward Taiwan, and ultimately our proposed policy prescriptions in the final sections of this report.[9]

I. ***China seeks to replace the United States as the most important and influential nation in the Indo-Pacific region and to dominate that region.*** This strategic goal may have been an aspiration among Chinese President Xi Jinping's recent predecessors, but it has become under Xi the engine of most of China's day-to-day foreign policies.[10] Convinced that the United States is in secular decline and the only questions being how fast and how far, Beijing projects its increasing economic and diplomatic power to undermine the foundations of the American posture in Asia, beginning with the U.S. alliance system.[11] As Lee Kuan Yew, late prime minister of Singapore and supreme global strategist, emphasized, "Why not? They have transformed a poor society by an economic miracle to become now the second-largest economy in the world—on track, as Goldman Sachs has predicted, to become the world's largest economy. . . . They have followed the American lead in putting people in space and shooting down satellites with missiles. Theirs is a culture 4,000 years old with 1.3 billion people, many of great talent—a huge and very talented pool to draw from. How could they not aspire to be number 1 in Asia, and in time the world?[12] . . . It is China's intention to be the greatest power in the world."[13]

2. *China's tactics will change over time; its desire for dominant influence, at least in the Indo-Pacific region, will not.* One sees this in the effective conciliatory speeches Xi and his senior colleagues make in international forums, which contrast vividly with former President Trump's bitter, resentful outbursts.[14] Indeed, Beijing remains a verbal champion of international cooperation precisely when the Trump administration largely abandoned it. This is not to say that China does not make mistakes in implementing its strategic goals through its tactical actions.[15] Its crude, threatening "wolf warrior" diplomacy is counterproductive. The financial terms of its Belt and Road Initiative have aggrieved some countries in the developing world.[16] China's military actions in the Himalayas along the India-China border in the early summer of 2020 in unforgiving mountain terrain have dramatically changed public opinion in India and pushed it geopolitically closer to the United States.[17] So this is far from an error-free team in Beijing.

3. *The crucial variable in whether China is successful in its strategic purpose is the domestic, economic, military, and diplomatic strength and resolve of the United States and its allies, and not Chinese actions.* At this writing, as the Biden administration enters office, the United States is deeply divided on political, economic, and racial issues, marked by a polarized Congress and an angry partisan public fed for years by Donald Trump's divisive rhetoric and actions exemplified by the chaos and violence at the Capitol in Washington on January 6. In this context, President Biden has an enormous challenge to unite the country in pursuit of agreed domestic and international goals. He will benefit from available vaccines and other medical

positives in the early months of his term that could lift some domestic pressure and give him more international flexibility. Should he succeed in reanimating American power and intensifying ties to allies, managing China's rise becomes substantially less daunting, and the leaders in Beijing would likely slow their aggressive push toward Asian dominance. Should he fail, he would only reinforce the view in Beijing and in some allied capitals that the United States has joined all the other nations over the centuries that dominated the international system, then faltered, then failed.

4. *The United States with its allies and partners can successfully compete with China, and there is no reason for intrinsic pessimism.* Although the following are not perfect comparisons, they are illustrative. The combined economies of the United States, Japan, South Korea, and Australia far outstrip that of China. U.S. nominal gross domestic product (GDP) in 2019 was $21.4 trillion compared to China's $14.3 trillion. The 2019 total nominal GDP of the United States, Japan, South Korea, and Australia was $29.5 trillion. When measured by purchasing power parity, China's $23.5 trillion GDP exceeds the U.S. figure of $21.4 trillion, but is still behind the $30.4 trillion of the U.S.-Asian alliances.[18] Even if the economic fallout of the coronavirus changed those numbers significantly for 2020, it is difficult to imagine that the immediate ramifications of the pandemic could close the GDP gap between China and the United States and its Asian allies. Additionally, PRC exports of goods and services in 2019 totaled $2.6 trillion, compared to $2.5 trillion in the United States, but U.S. allies in Asia make up almost $2 trillion in additional exports.[19]

Combined defense spending by the United States, Japan, South Korea, and Australia outpaced China in 2019. Washington spent $684.6 billion on defense and budgeted $69 billion for war funding. Japan, South Korea, and Australia combined to spend an additional $113.9 billion on defense. China, the second biggest spender, put an estimated $181.1 billion toward defense. That said, it is difficult to quantify or accurately break down PRC military expenditures, and Beijing does not pay as much per soldier as Washington does.[20] Of course, what matters most is what is being purchased in these budgets.

China has modernized its force at a blistering pace since 2000, but U.S. allies in Asia are also increasing budgets to acquire more advanced weapons and improve their navies' blue-water capabilities. The four now have advantages in most general military dimensions over China, including a U.S. superiority in naval tonnage, higher-quality submarines, and superior long-range stealth aircraft.[21] However, these sorts of measures of inputs shed relatively little light on who can sustain prolonged combat—and where. The PRC has major advantages in its ability to sustain fighting on a large scale in the seas and airspace near Taiwan.

Beijing often cannot match the united diplomacy of Washington and its allies and partners in Asia and Europe, but this situation is evolving. The United States and NATO allies the United Kingdom and France hold three of five of the permanent UN Security Council seats. Although China acquired chairmanship of four UN specialized agencies, the United States and its European and Asian allies combined hold chairmanship of six.[22] But China does not stand idle. It is strengthening its military partnership with Russia. It maintains close relations with Iran, Pakistan, Myanmar, and North Korea. All of these except North Korea have conducted joint military exercises in several locations. China, Russia, and Iran have carried out joint naval exercises. Russian and Chinese bombers have flown together in patrols over the Sea of Japan.[23] Moreover, PRC economic linkages and dependencies have a value that can influence and compel behavior even among U.S. allies, the Philippines being a case in point. For instance, China recently concluded both the Regional Comprehensive Economic Partnership in Asia, which includes all five U.S. Asian treaty allies and a bilateral investment treaty with the European Union (EU).[24]

Although China is catching up, the United States still generally leads in the application of advanced technologies.[25] Moreover, Beijing's soft power and values appeal only to governments with authoritarian tendencies. India, although not a treaty ally of the United States, increasingly sees its capacity to avoid intimidation from Beijing as linked to ever-closer relations with the West. Further, publics in the democracies now decisively see China as a threat to their values and well-being. In October 2020, a Pew poll showed that in twelve democracies in Europe and Asia, majorities of at least 70 percent had a very or somewhat unfavorable view of China. A report published in November 2020 by the Central European Institute of Asian Studies revealed that in all thirteen European nations surveyed, respondents had a negative view of China's "effect on democracy in other countries."[26] Finally, in addition to all these factors are the many substantial domestic problems China currently faces that will to some degree constrain its external behavior.[27] In short, there is much repair to be done with respect to U.S. international influence and America's alliance systems after the Trump years, but enormous potential power resides in these nations to work together to deal successfully with China.

5. **The United States and China are well on their way to confrontation, which could eventually lead to war.** During the past two years, almost every international issue divided Washington and Beijing. They disagreed about the most effective ideological underpinnings and political structures for modern societies, the futures of Hong Kong and Taiwan, freedom of navigation and the nature of maritime claims in the South China Sea, how best to curtail the North Korean and Iranian nuclear weapons programs, nuclear weapons and arms control, cyber penetration and other influence operations, the place of alliances in the current era, bilateral trade and intellectual property, human rights, 5G networks and advanced technology, climate change, China's Belt and Road Initiative and geoeconomic coercion, the India-China dispute in the Himalayas, and the proper roles and missions of international organizations. In the fervor of the just completed U.S. electoral season, many of these disagreements have worsened, a problematical reality that the Biden administration just inherited.

6. **In the past few years, Beijing and Washington seemed uninterested in using diplomacy to arrest the potentially catastrophic decline in their relations.** Few meetings have been held between the top diplomats of the two sides, and crisis management mechanisms are moribund.[28] Thus neither the United States nor China made any serious effort to reduce disagreements on the major issues between them. Instead, they hurled daily public accusations against the other. Secretary of State Mike Pompeo all but said that Washington could not successfully address its problems with Beijing as long as the Chinese Communist Party ruled there—in short, a call for regime change. China in its media has found nothing good to say about the United States, from its racial and class problems to its international behavior. This absence of diplomacy perplexes because it widens the U.S.-China gulf and increases the likelihood of eventual violent confrontation. History is replete with examples of how such conflict-ridden policies by contending states lead to tragedy. One hopes that the Biden administration will rectify this problem.

7. **No grand bargain will be struck between the United States and China on world order.** Dozens of such well-meaning formulae have been offered by distinguished analysts in the present public debate.[29] None is likely to work. The United States and China have different histories, political cultures, values, perceived national interests, long-term foreign policy goals, and visions of domestic and world order. This is

especially true given that both the U.S. and Chinese governments currently strive for illusionary primacy in the Indo-Pacific. Because each is seeking primary leadership in Asia, they will not reach a sustained and stable "grand bargain" about the region for the foreseeable future. Only quality diplomacy on both sides will rescue them from possible catastrophe. Only quality diplomacy, issue by issue, can slowly build possibilities for practical cooperation in addressing the common problems that have come, more and more, to mark this age of intense globalization and digital revolution.

As the great diplomatic historian Ernest May stressed, history provides the most common form of evidence and reasoning in forming public policy. It is filled with pertinent questions and insights—but not analogous policy prescriptions. In that spirit, Henry Kissinger observes that the current state of U.S.-China relations reminds him of the period before World War I, when Europe's leaders would not have made the decisions they did had they known the horrible consequences.

U.S.-TAIWAN POLICY EVOLVES

The island now known as Taiwan—formally the Republic of China (ROC)—was ruled by its indigenous inhabitants until the Dutch colonized part of the island between 1624 and 1668. The island became a short-lived kingdom of Ming dynasty generals driven out by the Qing conquerors in China until it was taken over by the Qing empire in 1688. The Qing remained for about two hundred years and fostered more settlement of the island from the mainland until they ceded Taiwan (then also commonly called Formosa) to Japan after the Sino-Japanese war of 1894–95. Taiwan remained under Japanese rule until 1945, when it was returned to Chinese rule by decision of the American, Chinese, and British leaders, announced in the Cairo Declaration of December 1943. The net result has been that, since 1895, Taiwan was under mainland rule only between 1945 and 1949.

After the Kuomintang (KMT) fled to Taiwan in 1949, and China entered the Korean War in the autumn of 1950, the United States joined in the illusion that the only legitimate government of China was in Taipei and regarded the fate of Taiwan as an open international question that, one way or another, should only be settled peacefully. In 1954, Washington, in the spirit of the intensifying Cold War, formalized military assistance to Taiwan with the Mutual Defense Treaty Between the United States and the Republic of China, which began decades of American support for the island.[30]

The next major evolution in U.S. policy toward Taiwan began in 1967 as former Vice President Richard M. Nixon observed that "we simply cannot afford to leave China forever outside the family of nations."[31] After Nixon became president, he dispatched Henry Kissinger in July 1971 on a secret visit to thaw relations between the United States and China and to discuss the primary concerns of the two sides. For

Washington, those were to balance the power of the Soviet Union and end the Vietnam War. Beijing sought American agreement that Taiwan was an indelible part of China.

Nixon realized that normalization of U.S.-PRC relations would upset Taipei. In June 1971, he told the U.S. ambassador to the ROC that "we must have in mind, and they must be prepared for the fact, that there will continue to be a step-by-step, a more normal relationship with the other—the Chinese mainland. Because our interests require it. Not because we love them, but because they're there."[32] When Nixon surprised the world with a televised announcement in July of that year that he would travel to China, he stressed that warmer U.S.-China relations would "not be at the expense of our old friends."[33]

In February 1972, after intense negotiation during the Nixon visit, Washington and Beijing issued a joint statement in Shanghai—the first of the Three Communiques that have provided the scaffolding for U.S. policy affecting Taiwan and China over the decades. In this first communique, a profound compromise between Washington and Beijing noted that "the United States acknowledges that all Chinese on either side of the Taiwan Strait maintain there is but one China and that Taiwan is a part of China. The United States Government does not challenge that position."[34]

In 1979, in the second communique, the Carter administration established diplomatic relations with Beijing and acknowledged "the Chinese position that there is but one China and Taiwan is part of China," recognized the PRC "as the sole legal Government of China," and stated that "the people of the United States will maintain cultural, commercial, and other unofficial relations with the people of Taiwan."[35] In short, Washington cut official ties with Taipei to establish relations with Beijing.

After much of Congress objected to what it perceived as this U.S. abandonment of Taiwan, the Carter administration then proposed in 1979 the Taiwan Enabling Act as a roadmap for unofficial relations with Taiwan. However, it did not receive the necessary approval from U.S. lawmakers.[36] Congress instead passed the stronger 1979 Taiwan Relations Act (TRA) with veto-proof majorities, which were enough to convince the president to sign the bill into law. The TRA, among other things, states that it is U.S. policy to "consider any effort to determine the future of Taiwan by other than peaceful means, including by boycotts or embargoes, a threat to the peace and security of the Western Pacific area and of grave concern to the United States"; "to maintain the capacity of the United States to resist any resort to force or other forms of coercion that would jeopardize the security, or the social or economic system, of the people on Taiwan"; to provide defensive arms to Taipei; and to maintain cultural and commercial ties between the American and Taiwanese people. It also laid out procedures for applying U.S. laws to Taiwan and established the American Institute in Taiwan (AIT) as a congressionally chartered quasi-embassy.[37]

On August 17, 1982, the United States, then led by President Ronald Reagan, and China issued the final of the Three Communiques. This document noted the PRC position that "the question of Taiwan is China's internal affair"; stated that Washington had "no intention of infringing on Chinese sovereignty and territorial integrity, or interfering in China's internal affairs, or pursuing a policy of 'two Chinas' or 'one China, one Taiwan'"; and said that the United States would seek "gradually to reduce its sale of arms to Taiwan, leading, over a period of time, to a final resolution."[38]

That same summer, Reagan administration officials wrote two now-declassified cables that clarified the U.S. view of relations with Taiwan. A July message from Undersecretary of State Lawrence Eagleburger to AIT Director James Lilley stressed that reduced U.S. arms sales to Taiwan were "premised on a continuation of the Chinese policy of seeking a peaceful resolution of the Taiwan issue."[39] Then, on August 17, the day the third U.S.-China communique was issued, Secretary of State George Shultz instructed Lilley to convey the Six Assurances to the Taiwan government that the United States

- "has not agreed to set a date for ending arms sales to Taiwan";

- "has not agreed to consult with the PRC on arms sales to Taiwan";

- "will not play any mediation role between Taipei and Beijing";

- "has not agreed to revise the Taiwan Relations Act";

- "has not altered its position regarding sovereignty over Taiwan"; and

- "will not exert pressure on Taiwan to enter into negotiations with the PRC."[40]

Statements and actions during the Clinton presidency were a microcosm of the balancing act required by U.S. policy affecting Taiwan and China. In 1994, the administration presented the results of its Taiwan Policy Review, a comprehensive examination of the U.S. stance toward the island. Washington announced that it was "prepared to send high-level officials from U.S. economic and technical agencies to visit Taiwan," that it would change the name of the Taiwanese counterpart to AIT from the Coordination Council for North American Affairs to the Taipei Economic and Cultural Representative Office (TECRO), and that Taiwanese officials would be allowed to transit through the United States "consistent with security and comfort and convenience."[41]

When Taiwanese President Lee Teng-hui accepted an invitation to attend an event at Cornell University in 1995, the Clinton administration opposed the trip on the grounds that such a visit would overstep the bounds of the unofficial relationship between the United States and Taiwan. The administration relented after Congress voted overwhelmingly in support of the visit.[42] Beijing responded by firing missiles into the waters off Taiwan after Lee's visit and again before Taiwan's first presidential election in 1996, prompting the dispatch of American aircraft carriers to the Taiwan Strait to demonstrate dominating American military strength. After the crisis, Secretary of State Warren Christopher urged cross-strait stability and declared, "We have emphasized to both sides the importance of avoiding provocative actions or unilateral measures that would alter the status quo or pose a threat to peaceful resolution of outstanding issues."[43] Clinton in 1998 articulated what is known as the Three Nos when he announced, "we don't support independence for Taiwan, or two Chinas, or one Taiwan-one China. And we don't believe that Taiwan should be a member in any organization for which statehood is a requirement."[44]

As President George W. Bush took office in 2001, the election the year before of Taiwanese President Chen Shui-bian of the independence-leaning Democratic Progressive Party (DPP) made for tense cross-strait relations. The Bush administration (as well as the administrations that followed) also publicly recognized Taiwan's importance as a major U.S.

trading partner and a crucial player in the world's information technology supply chain, not simply as a troublesome issue in Washington's relationship with Beijing.[45] In January 2002, following groundwork laid by the Clinton administration, Taiwan joined the World Trade Organization (WTO) under the name of Separate Customs Territory of Taiwan, Penghu, Kinmen and Matsu. Mainland China had entered the group one month earlier.[46] Taiwan was admitted because membership is not limited to nations; China's entrance was conditioned on Taiwan's.

Bush, like his predecessors, was keen to maintain restraint on both sides of the Taiwan Strait. At a 2002 news conference, he pronounced that the "'one China policy' means the issue ought to be resolved peacefully."[47] When in 2003 Washington worried that President Chen's proposed referendum on PRC missiles pointed toward Taiwan could be a precedent for a similar poll on independence, Bush declared that "the comments and actions made by the leader of Taiwan indicate that he may be willing to make decisions unilaterally, to change the status quo, which we oppose."[48] Cross-strait relations once again grew precarious when Beijing passed the 2005 Anti-Secession Law, which allowed the PRC to use "non-peaceful means" to prevent Taiwan independence in certain circumstances. Bush the same year said in an interview that "if China were to invade unilaterally, we would rise up in the spirit of [the] Taiwan Relations Act. If Taiwan were to declare independence unilaterally, it would be a unilateral decision that would then change the U.S. equation."[49]

The Obama administration sold Taiwan advanced PAC-3 missile defense batteries and notified a significant F-16 upgrade that brought Taiwan's force up to the level of the most advanced F-16 configuration. However, it refused to sell new F-16s to the island in 2011 despite bipartisan legislation in support of the deal.[50] Obama's time in office largely coincided with the Beijing-friendly KMT party President Ma Ying-jeou's tenure in Taiwan. During these years, the United States sent only one to three ships per year through the Taiwan Strait, allowed Taiwan to participate in the U.S. Visa Waiver Program, signed legislation to sell Taiwan four used missile frigates, and permitted TECRO to hold a celebration at Twin Oaks, the former Washington residence of the ROC ambassador to the United States.[51]

Thus, over the decades, Washington's administration pronouncements, congressional actions, and diplomatic cables coalesced into a U.S. One China policy that, as Bonnie S. Glaser and Michael J. Green authoritatively stress, "recognizes the PRC as the sole legal government of China but only acknowledges the Chinese position that Taiwan is part of China. Thus, the United States maintains formal relations with the PRC and has unofficial relations with Taiwan."[52] In short, no U.S. policy of two Chinas or of one China, one Taiwan.

When then President-Elect Trump spoke on the phone with Taiwanese President Tsai Ing-wen in December 2016, Obama said the incoming Trump administration was within its rights to review the One China policy, but stressed that the "status quo, although not completely satisfactory to any of the parties involved, has kept the peace and allowed the Taiwanese to be a pretty successful . . . economy and a people who have a high degree of self-determination." Obama cautioned that outside of U.S.-China relations "there's probably no bilateral relationship that carries more significance and . . . where there's also the potential, if that relationship breaks down or goes into a full conflict mode, that everybody is worse off."[53]

The Trump administration raised U.S. support for Taiwan higher than at any time since 1971.[54] It reversed Obama administration policy and helped finalize the 2020 sale of sixty-six F-16s to Taiwan.[55] The administration shuffled responsibilities of the deputy assistant secretaries of defense (DASD) to add Taiwan to the portfolio of the DASD for East Asia responsible for U.S. partners and allies in the Pacific, rather than to a DASD for mainland China. Public and private visits by U.S. and Taiwanese officials grew in profile. The Trump administration allowed President Tsai to stay for two days each way on her 2019 transit through the United States in a break from the usual one-day stopover policy, and when Health and Human Services Secretary Alex Azar stopped in Taipei in August 2020, he became the highest-ranking U.S. government official to visit the island in decades.[56] One month later, U.S. Undersecretary of State for Economic Growth, Energy, and the Environment Keith Krach attended the funeral of former Taiwanese President Lee Teng-hui; in November 2020, U.S. Rear Admiral Michael Studeman traveled unannounced to the island; and on January 9, 2021, Secretary of State Pompeo removed all restrictions governing interaction between the U.S. and Taiwan governments.[57] The president also signed the FY2017 National Defense Authorization Act, which encouraged the secretary of defense to "carry out a program of exchanges of senior military officers"; the 2018 Taiwan Travel Act, which said the U.S. government should promote "visits between officials from the United States and Taiwan at all levels"; and the 2020 Taiwan Assurance Act, which urged regular arms sales to Taiwan.[58] U.S. Navy ships also increased their transits.[59]

The Biden administration immediately tried to strike in its policy toward Taiwan a new balance. As we mentioned at the beginning of the report, the administration, notably in its January 23 statement, has stressed sympathy for Taiwan while reaffirming the "longstanding commitments" of the United States, "as outlined in the Three Communiques, the Taiwan Relations Act, and the Six Assurances." It pledged only to "continue to assist Taiwan in maintaining a sufficient self-defense capability," while stressing that "our commitment to Taiwan is rock-solid."

TAIWAN RISES

Taiwan is one of the most successful societies on Earth. Unlike dozens of nations, it is now a flourishing democracy. Unlike dozens of nations, it is governed by rule of law. Unlike dozens of nations, it holds free and fair elections. Unlike dozens of nations, it protects the political and human rights of its citizens. Unlike dozens of nations, it has an unfettered and competitive media. Unlike dozens of nations, it endorses religious diversity. Unlike dozens of nations, it is a responsible international actor. It also has a population of twenty-three million, larger than most nations.

Including its first direct presidential vote in 1996, Taiwan has held seven presidential elections with minimal irregularities. Voters have transferred power back and forth from the KMT—which ran the island under martial law and for a period thereafter—to the DPP. Taiwan ranks just behind South Korea and ahead of the United States in press freedom and has instituted a society-wide effort to combat false or misleading claims through education programs, an independent online list of disproven conspiracy theories, laws to combat foreign influence efforts, and algorithms that focus on consensus rather than division in internet conversations.[60] Taiwanese citizens are enthusiastic about their governing system. The 2020 presidential elections saw a 75 percent voter turnout.[61] In a survey that same year, 79.7 percent of those polled said that democracy, though flawed, was the best system of government for Taiwan. Additionally, 63 percent said they were optimistic about their democracy—an increase of 19.9 percent from 2019.[62]

Although the pandemic sent democracies and illiberal regimes alike scrambling to avoid economic rupture, Taiwan was one of a small group of societies to end 2020 with positive real GDP growth and projects a 2.5 percent increase in 2020.[63] Its exports in 2020 were the highest in the history of its economy.[64] Many of the trends that made Taiwan successful in 2020 are likely to continue. As more people around the world rely on technology to work and be entertained from home, Taiwan's electronics and manufacturing sectors are expected to rise to meet increased global demand and buttress the economy for the immediate future.[65]

Taiwan's dominance in chip manufacturing means it possesses a component essential to the American, Chinese, and the global economies.[66] A continuation of the U.S.-China trade confrontation remains a risk, but economic forecasts for Taiwan from late 2020 project GDP growth for 2021 to exceed 3 percent and continued positive growth through at least 2025.[67]

At the same time, strong economic performance and an effective response to the coronavirus pandemic should not distract from vulnerabilities that could threaten Taipei's sustained economic success. Although Taiwan dominates the market for cutting-edge semiconductor chips, it lags in the software expertise needed to make full use of its lead in advanced hardware and especially in fields that place a premium on the integration of the two. Application of Taiwanese chip technology largely takes place abroad, and Taiwan is not positioned to merge software and hardware at home.[68] In 2019, Taiwan had nearly 76,000 students enrolled in university programs for math, statistics, information, and communication technologies compared to 163,000 in engineering and manufacturing and processing-related fields.[69]

Of further concern is that the Taiwanese population shrank by 0.2 percent in 2020.[70] The aging island is on the demographic path to 20 percent of the population older than sixty-five by 2025 and faces associated challenges to the workforce, government accounts, and military service.[71] All of this combined with labor and land scarcity, talent migration to mainland China and the United States, government initiatives such as the 5+2 Innovative Industries Plan that have yet to yield significant results, and a start-up ecosystem too focused on Taiwan's relatively small market pose formidable hurdles.[72]

Nevertheless, many countries would be delighted to have Taiwan's economic advantages. A high-tech and sophisticated business culture, a hardworking and disciplined workforce, and internal political stability promise Taiwan's continued economic growth and increased prosperity.

Volatile cross-strait relations in Taiwan's early years did not guarantee that Taiwan would have the stability and prosperity that draw so much praise today. War seemed imminent at times during the reign of Chiang Kai-shek. Banners reading "Recover the Mainland" hung over Taiwanese roads.[73] In a 1956 discussion with U.S. Assistant Secretary of

State Walter Robertson, Chiang said that "it would be difficult to return to China right now; however, it would be impossible to maintain status quo eternally. Therefore, within several years, I would like to return to China. It will take some time, and the U.S. support will be absolutely important."[74] Lack of American endorsement, though, contributed to Taiwan's never launching an invasion.

Chiang Kai-shek's son Chiang Ching-kuo came to power in May 1978 shortly before the United States cut diplomatic relations with Taiwan, and quickly articulated a policy of Three Nos—no contact, no negotiation, and no compromise with China. However, in the years before his death in 1988, the younger Chiang both opened links with the PRC—which allowed Taiwanese citizens to visit relatives on the mainland—and moved Taiwan toward democratization. Democracy, he understood, would shore up American support.[75]

Chiang's successor Lee Teng-hui emphasized a separate Taiwanese identity, which complicated cross-strait relations. His statement that Taipei and Beijing had a "special state-to-state relationship" did not win him favor on the mainland.[76]

When DPP candidate Chen Shui-ban came to power in 2000, the first non-KMT president in Taiwan's history was careful to project a moderate tone early in his presidency. Chen's inauguration speech emphasized shared traits between Taiwanese and Chinese and said "as long as the CCP [Chinese Communist Party] regime has no intention to use military force against Taiwan, I pledge that during my term in office, I will not declare independence, I will not change the national title, I will not push forth the inclusion of the so-called 'state-to-state' description in the Constitution, and I will not promote a referendum to change the status quo in regard to the question of independence or unification."[77] Despite sharp protest from both Washington and Beijing, Chen did call for a referendum in 2004, which included language on PRC missiles directed at Taiwan and cross-strait negotiations. The United States and China both worried this was a step toward a pro-independence referendum, but the results were voided on the basis of inadequate turnout.[78]

KMT candidate Ma Ying-jeou's election in 2008 saw a considerable warming of trade, increased travel, and more frequent communication between the two sides. In his first inaugural address, Ma said that Taiwan would "enter consultations with mainland China over Taiwan's international space and a possible cross-strait peace accord."[79] However, in the later years of his presidency, Ma faced pressure from the Taiwanese people, who did not always appreciate his cooperation with

Beijing. This culminated in the 2014 Sunflower Movement, when student activists occupied the Legislative Yuan in protest of a free services trade agreement with China, which never went into effect.[80]

When DPP candidate Tsai Ing-wen came to office in 2016, anti-mainland sentiment was on the rise in Taiwan. Despite Tsai's efforts to subtly reassure China of her aversion to declaring independence—her promise to adhere to the ROC constitution and laws governing cross-strait relations insinuated that she would not formally separate from the mainland—formal communication with China was, and remains, infrequent.[81]

Amid this backdrop, Taiwanese public opinion of China does not portend well for unification or a more conciliatory policy toward the mainland. Promisingly, Taiwan does not appear in favor of a wholesale abandonment of cross-strait dialogue. According to one survey, 76.9 percent of Taiwanese people approve or strongly approve of continuing people-to-people exchanges with China if the pandemic threat passes; 85.3 percent support or strongly support engagement with Beijing "while parity and dignity are maintained," not least because of the Taiwan business community's investments on the mainland.[82] China itself though is exceedingly unpopular in Taiwan. The latest Pew polls show that 61 percent of adults have an unfavorable view of the PRC.[83] Unification on Beijing's terms is met with a similar lack of enthusiasm. Approximately 1 percent of Taiwanese support unification immediately and more than 60 percent are against unification under "one country, two systems."[84]

Meanwhile, the warming of U.S.-Taiwan relations under the Tsai and Trump administrations has promoted U.S. standing on the island. A poll conducted by Taipei's Mainland Affairs Council showed that 73.4 percent of respondents approve of stronger U.S.-Taiwan engagement to bolster defense and security and a Pew survey revealed that 85 percent are in favor of closer U.S.-Taiwan economic ties.[85] In the same Pew study, more than two-thirds of participants expressed a favorable view of the United States—nearly double the number of those who see China in a positive light.[86] Of note is the confidence Taiwanese citizens have in U.S. willingness to use force to respond to a Chinese attack. According to a 2020 survey, more than 60 percent expect American aid if Taiwan suffers an unprovoked attack, but 53.2 percent expect the United States to fight in support of Taiwan if the island declares independence.[87]

CHINA CONFRONTS TAIWAN

China's policy that Taiwan is part of the PRC has been nothing if not strategically consistent.[88] Beijing intended to annex Taiwan immediately after the end of the Chinese Civil War, but the outbreak of the Korean War in 1950 and the 1954 U.S.-Taiwan mutual defense treaty put those plans on hold.[89] When China sought to improve relations with the United States in the early 1970s, the Taiwan issue was a top priority for Beijing. As Zhou Enlai claimed to Henry Kissinger, "Taiwan has belonged to China for more than 1000 years. . . . Taiwan is a Chinese province, is already restored to China, and is an inalienable part of Chinese territory."[90]

Deng Xiaoping viewed Taiwan as a natural economic partner and believed that deepening cross-strait economic ties would eventually pave the road to "peaceful reunification" under the One Country, Two Systems framework also being idealized for the future of Hong Kong.[91] Deng also made clear that the use of force in principle was a live option for Beijing: "We are pursuing a policy of 'one country, two systems.' . . . If the problem cannot be solved by peaceful means, then it must be solved by force."[92]

After Tiananmen Square and the fall and splintering of the Soviet Union, Jiang Zemin and his colleagues became more worried about Taiwan and its increasingly separate identity.[93] Although the two political parties, the KMT and the CCP, came to a partial agreement—the so-called 1992 Consensus—that there was One China, they differed on the meaning of the term. And amid rising tensions and in advance of Taiwan's first direct presidential election in 1996, China launched missiles toward Taiwan's adjoining waters. As foreign ministry spokesman Shen Guofang stressed on March 15, 1996, "China has never promised to abstain from resorting to arms."[94] To again reinforce that point, in 2005 China passed the Anti-Secession Law, which stated that China could use "non-peaceful means" if Taiwan secessionist forces sought independence or if it deemed that possibilities of peaceful reunification were "completely exhausted." This language is significant: many on both sides of the strait now believe that that situation has already been reached.[95]

When KMT politician Ma Ying-jeou won the Taiwanese presidency in 2008, Beijing took a more conciliatory policy than it did under Ma's DPP predecessor Chen Shui-bian. Beijing resumed cross-strait exchanges with Taipei, cooperated with Ma to strengthen economic ties and advanced a number of agreements that increased cross-strait flights and boosted the flow of mainland tourists to Taiwan, lowered regulations and tariffs on cross-strait trade, and allowed Taiwan's participation in select international bodies and forums such as the World Health Assembly (WHA). However, this coincided with rising anti-Chinese sentiment in Taiwan. Ma's domestic popularity faded and Taiwan's citizens reacted to Xi's increased focus on the One China principle.[96] Xi Jinping stressed to a senior Taiwanese envoy in October 2013 that a political solution to cross-strait relations could not be postponed forever.[97]

This relatively harmonious PRC policy toward Taiwan changed abruptly when DPP stalwart Tsai Ing-wen was elected president in 2016. In June of that year, China ended official contact with Taiwan because of what it asserted was President Tsai's noncommitment to One China.[98] Since 2016 China has also

- selectively enforced agreements with Taiwan;

- made it more difficult for DPP-sympathetic scholars and business leaders to work in China;

- worked to push Taiwan out of the international system and reduce its diplomatic allies;

- coerced foreign businesses to refer to Taiwan as part of China;

- cut all official cross-strait exchanges, reduced the flow of Chinese group tourists, and banned individual travel by Chinese citizens to the island;

- prevented Taiwan from participating in bodies such as the World Health Organization (WHO) and the UN International Civil Aviation Organization (ICAO); and

- significantly increased its military intimidation of Taiwan.[99]

Beijing will not accept from Taiwan anything other than explicit acceptance of Beijing's interpretation of the 1992 Consensus, which Tsai has refused to do.[100] In China's view, the One Country, Two Systems framework applied to Taiwan would mean that

- the Republic of China would no longer exist;

- the PRC would absorb Taiwan and the PRC flag would fly over Taiwan;

- Taiwan would become a special administrative region like Hong Kong and Macau;

- Beijing would take charge of Taiwanese foreign and defense policy;

- Taiwan's economy and society would continue to exist in their present state;

- Taiwan would maintain its own army, China would not station troops in Taiwan, and the United States would not project military force toward China from Taiwan; and

- China would decide how Taiwan's leaders are chosen and would not allow certain leaders to be selected.[101]

It is no surprise that these conditions are unacceptable to any conceivable Taiwan government. In a January 2020 speech, Tsai Ing-wen stressed that "as president of the Republic of China, I must solemnly emphasize that we have never accepted the '1992 Consensus'... because the Beijing authorities' definition of the '1992 Consensus' is 'one China' and 'one country, two systems.'"[102]

This brings us to today and Beijing's future policies toward Taiwan. Because those policies are considered and decided behind closed doors, we have to speculate. However, it would be surprising if the Chinese leadership did not notice the following regarding Taiwan:

- China's mix of incentives and coercion over seven decades has linked the economies of the island and the mainland but produced no movement toward Taiwan unification.

- The Chinese will notice that trends now in Taiwan are all toward separation, fed by Xi's behavior, the fate of Hong Kong, and the strength of Taiwan's democratic institutions. In Taiwan's 2020 presidential election, Tsai Ing-wen won reelection with 57 percent of the vote, one of the biggest electoral victories in the history of Taiwanese democracy.[103] A survey released by Pew in May 2020 showed that 66 percent of adults in Taiwan identify as Taiwanese, 28 percent identify as Taiwanese and Chinese, and 4 percent see themselves only as Chinese.[104]

- The fate of Hong Kong has in Taiwan irreparably ended One Country, Two Systems as a viable model for peaceful integration into the mainland.[105]

- Taiwan's vibrant democratic system could eventually become an alternative—and thus a threat—to the communist system on the mainland.[106]

- Taiwan's successful mitigation of the coronavirus has strengthened its international standing, especially with Japan and Australia, two U.S. Pacific treaty allies.

- Support for Taiwan is now stronger in the United States than in many decades, including in Congress and by the American public. Congress passed the Taiwan Travel Act in 2018, and the TAIPEI Act and Taiwan Assurance Act in 2020, to strengthen U.S.-Taiwan relations.[107] Fifteen Republican and nine Democratic senators make up the Senate Taiwan Caucus, and sixty-two Republicans and fifty-eight Democrats are part of the group's counterpart in the House.[108] A poll conducted in July and August of 2020 by the Center for Strategic and International Studies used a ten-point scale to gauge willingness to defend allies. It revealed that the American public was more eager to defend Taiwan (an average response of 6.69) than Australia (6.38). Appetites for defending Japan (6.88), South Korea (6.92), or an unspecified partner in the South China Sea (6.97) were also comparable to results on Taiwan.[109]

- The Biden administration will seek to strengthen U.S. alliances and its power projection into the Asia-Pacific in order to increase deterrence against a PRC attack on Taiwan. The United States will become better positioned and more influential in the region than in recent years.

- Time does not appear to be on China's side regarding the integration of Taiwan into the mainland, unless the timeline is decades to a century to a millennium.

- It is now hard to imagine Taiwan reunification with China without a successful use of force or massive nonviolent coercion by Beijing, unless the PRC profoundly changes its political system.[110]

One can perhaps see Xi's frustration in a speech he gave on January 2, 2019, commemorating the fortieth anniversary of the Message to Compatriots in Taiwan: "We will work with the greatest sincerity and exert utmost efforts to achieve peaceful reunification, because this works best for the people on both sides and for our whole nation. We do not renounce the use of force and reserve the option of taking all necessary measures."[111]

In 2019, for the first time in two decades, People's Liberation Army (PLA) aircraft breached the median line, an unofficial boundary between two sides in the Taiwan Strait. In the months after a series of high-level meetings between U.S. and Taiwanese officials in September 2020, Beijing sent dozens of aircraft across the line.[112] Chinese propaganda organs increased the bellicosity of rhetoric toward Taiwan in videos of drills featuring amphibious landing craft, statements from Beijing's Taiwan Affairs Office that the "root cause for cross-strait tensions is the DPP leadership that refuses to recognize ... the one-China principle," and *Global Times* commentary that "continued military muscle-flexing is the only answer to cross-strait stability."[113] Chinese Premier Li Keqiang and State Councilor Wang Yi avoided a reference to peaceful reunification when speaking in May 2020 at the National People's Congress, although the government-approved report of proceedings reintroduced the term.[114]

Xi Jinping may not have decided whether to take an even harder line toward Taiwan, but his tolerance for risk is demonstrated by China's aggressive stance on territorial disputes in the South China Sea, and with India and Japan.[115] At the same time, Xi is careful to avoid articulating a specific deadline for reunification, and his statements indicate a desire to make progress, but not necessarily a need to rush the issue.[116]

In any case, China will calculate its national interests carefully if it does decide to use force against Taiwan absent a crossing of one of China's red lines, and good reasons not to use force are numerous. As discussed in detail later, a PRC attack on Taiwan would disrupt Xi's plans for domestic renewal, weaken China's global standing, likely lead to substantial international sanctions, promote a global anti-China coalition, and could lead to war with the United States. Further, the PLA might not win quickly, or at all. Nevertheless, the PRC tends to favor worst-case scenarios and could respond harshly to what it regards as provocative actions by the United States or Taiwan.[117] History is full of such miscalculations that lead to war.

THREE SCENARIOS
FOR A MILITARY
CONFLICT OVER TAIWAN

Before going further, both of us wish to stress that, in preparing this report, we have not had access to or made any use of classified national security information of the United States.[118]

The prevailing assumption among experts we respect is that China would try to coerce Taiwan into a more pliable posture, but that this coercion probably would not be violent. China has many ways to harass Taiwan, measures that could increase the pain for all segments of Taiwan's society and signal that these costs could be eased only by adopting a stance that China regards as more deferential, less separatist. China could signal to Japan or South Korea, and others, that if they join others in confronting China, they could no longer count on the trade, security, and peace to which are accustomed. China could start blacklisting enterprises that do business in or with Taiwan or with certain enterprises in Taiwan.

These measures could grow into more dangerous forms of harassment, such as interruptions in commerce or cyberattacks or worse. Those who have followed the recent history of China's crackdown in Hong Kong can see an illustration of the pattern.

We are not sure these coercive measures would accomplish the PRC's goals vis-à-vis Taiwan. China's incremental steps in Hong Kong (and Xinjiang) did not appear to have met PRC objectives, and Beijing had to eventually wield the hammer. It is unclear whether Taiwan's citizens would react to such coercive measures by voting for the KMT, and whether the KMT's leaders would want to exploit such Chinese coercion.

But, if these experts are right and China does not use violence to achieve its objectives, then so much the better. That policy problem has been widely discussed in public and is different from the ones we primarily devote ourselves to in this report. It is the kind of incremental pressure and tension that U.S. and allied policymakers are more accustomed to handling. We hope that China judges that the costs of a violent confrontation would be too high, compared to the benefits.

Nevertheless, we believe that the odds of other scenarios are high enough that they now warrant immediate serious attention. To put it another way, how high would the odds of catching a deadly illness need to be before you would pay high costs—even undertake preventive surgery—to head off or meet the danger?

China is now in a prewar tempo of political and military preparations. We do not mean that we know that China is about to embark on a war. We simply observe that the Chinese government is taking actions that a country would do if it were moving into a prewar mode. Politically, it is preparing and conditioning its population for the possibility of an armed conflict. Militarily, it is engaging now in a tempo of exercises and military preparations that are both sharpening and widening the readiness of its armed forces across a range of different contingencies on sea, air, land, cyber, or in space. As true of the Israeli misreading of Egypt's intentions in the immediate period before the outbreak of the 1973 Yom Kippur War, this level of operational activity also complicates the work of foreign intelligence agencies and makes it much harder for them to distinguish ominous signals from the background noise.

All three scenarios we describe are alternative futures in which the Chinese government has decided to use military instruments to demonstrate or establish sovereign Chinese control over Taiwan.

China is already engaged in a campaign of constant military harassment at the edges of territory under Taiwanese control. These activities are often referred to as gray zone conflict. For example, Chinese aircraft enter Taiwan's air defense identification zone, obliging Taiwan to send up fighter aircraft—then the intruders return to Chinese airspace. Or Chinese ships do the same, forcing Taiwan's navy or coast guard to respond.[119]

The question, though, is what China is actually trying to accomplish. It allows Chinese forces to exercise themselves at Taiwan's expense. It can strain and exhaust Taiwan's air crew and sailors. It can force Taiwan to spend more money on fuel and maintenance. It can aggravate Taiwan's citizens and condition them to the idea that China is unhappy and aggressive. None of this really demonstrates Chinese authority or advances the possibility of a peaceful reunification of China with Taiwan. From a military point of view, these are all preliminaries.

To take this concept even further, China could decide to more tangibly demonstrate its power by invading one or another offshore island controlled by Taiwan. Within this scenario are four kinds of choices. The first, starting farthest away from mainland China, would be Taiwan-controlled Taiping Island (see figure 1). Other entities give it other names. This island is in the Spratly group, in the South China Sea, about equidistant between southern Vietnam and the Philippines.

A second possibility is the Pratas Islands. These are more of an atoll and are also called Dongsha. They are much closer to China and Taiwan. If one were to draw a straight line from Hong Kong directly to the Luzon Strait, between the northern edge of the Philippines and Taiwan, Pratas atoll lies along that line, about halfway to the strait. Thus the location of the Pratas Islands has some modest strategic value for the Chinese, given that it is on the way from Hong Kong or Hainan Island to the Luzon Strait and its Bashi Channel, which is one of the principal Chinese outlets to the deep Pacific.

A third possibility is the Penghu Islands, also known as the Pescadores. These are closer to southern Taiwan. Then, right off the shore of mainland China itself, is Kinmen, which is close to Xiamen, and Matsu, which is off the shore near Fuzhou. On these last two possibilities, either the Penghu Islands or Kinmen and Matsu, are significant permanent resident populations of thousands of people.

Taiping is relatively far away in the already contested South China Sea. Pratas does not have a permanent population. At least since August

Figure 1: EAST CHINA AND TAIWAN

SOUTH KOREA

JAPAN

CHINA

EAST CHINA SEA

Ryukyu Islands

Matsu

Fuzhou ●

Taiwan Strait

Xiamen ●   ● Taipei

Guangzhou ● Shantou ●   **TAIWAN**

● Kinmen

HONG KONG   Penghu ● Kaohsiung

Bashi Channel

Pratas   *Luzon Strait*

Hainan

SOUTH CHINA SEA

VIETNAM

PHILIPPINES

Taiping —

Spratly Islands

2020, however, Taiwan has deployed hundreds of soldiers to defend Pratas.[120] The Chinese have been conducting frequent overflights and exercises in the vicinity of this atoll.

Of these four kinds of choices, Pratas would seem to be the most tempting for Beijing, if it were undefended. Probably noticing this, Taiwan is now defending it. Thus, the first big question in this scenario of

China invading the offshore islands, in any of the four cases, is whether the Taiwanese defenders will actually fight or immediately capitulate.

Those who favor World War II analogies could think of Wake Island. When the Japanese attacked in December 1941 after Pearl Harbor, the Marines and others on Wake Island fought hard. It was a doomed fight, but they battled, and the fact that they battled made a difference. It helped catalyze and further rally the already roused American public. If the Taiwanese fight and casualties are significant, it would have a large political effect in Taiwan, in Japan, in the United States, and elsewhere.

Another big question is, if a fight were to break out, would the Taiwanese *extend* it? Imagine a conflict over Pratas, for example, that engages the several hundred defenders there and is not over in minutes. The Taiwanese would have to decide whether to send more forces. For instance, Taipei would have to decide whether to use its submarines, surface vessels, or aircraft to interfere with the Chinese attack force. Those reinforcements would raise the stakes and extend the conflict. If that happened, more bloodshed and clamor would follow, which also would have important regional and global political implications.

We have no idea what the Taiwanese plans are in this scenario. We would be surprised if the U.S. government were confident that it knew what these plans are. Then again, we are not sure Taiwan's government itself now knows exactly what it would do.

Superficially, to Chinese planners, an attack on offshore islands could look like a relatively low-risk activity. They would have high confidence that, militarily, they can take the island that they choose. But, again, the question comes back to what China is really trying to accomplish. The Chinese would not have settled the underlying issue of Taiwan's sovereignty; they would have only aggravated it. They would have only demonstrated overwhelming strength on a peripheral part of the issue.

The PRC could then pay a high cost in this scenario while achieving relatively little. Beijing could imagine it would teach Taiwan a lesson. But if the Taiwanese fight, and their battle had a large political blowback in Taiwan and around the world, the Chinese government could find that it had now militarized the otherwise divided, ambivalent population of Taiwan and spurred Japanese, American, and other interventions. Thus, in this scenario, the Chinese could pay a significant long-term cost without having resolved the core issue. However, we stress that, like the other scenarios in this report, Beijing's calculations could be different from ours.

SCENARIO 2: CHINA QUARANTINES TAIWAN

By quarantine, we do not mean blockade. In a quarantine scenario, the Chinese government would effectively take control of the air and sea borders of Taiwan. It would declare control over Taiwan's airspace so that, in effect, Taipei's Taoyuan International Airport was no longer its own international gateway, and Kaohsiung was no longer its own international port. The Chinese government would run effectively a clearance operation offshore or in the air to screen incoming ships and aircraft. The screeners could then wave along what they regarded as innocent traffic. Or they could request that suspect ships or aircraft divert for full Chinese customs clearance at a neighboring airport on the mainland or in a neighboring port, such as Fuzhou or Guangzhou, or Xiamen or Shantou. China has excellent "domain awareness," having plenty of ships from its navy, coast guard, and maritime militia at its disposal to accomplish this task.

On January 22, 2021, the Chinese government's National People's Congress passed a new law governing its coast guard. This law expressly authorized coast guard ships to use "all necessary means" against foreign vessels, and to board and inspect such vessels in waters claimed by China. The bill empowered the coast guard to create temporary exclusion zones "as needed" to keep other vessels from entering.[121]

The Chinese government could make two kinds of arguments to defend such a quarantine. First, of course, is that it is affirming and establishing sovereign control over Taiwan. Given that much of the world has nominally conceded that there is only one China, and therefore has arguably accepted that China has some sort of sovereign rights over Taiwan, the Chinese government could assert that it is both confirming and asserting those rights.

The Chinese government could run such a quarantine without actually trying to take effective control of the Taiwanese people themselves. In this scenario, the Chinese government would allow the people in Taiwan to run their own affairs on the island, at least for some time, as China showed that it controlled who came (and perhaps who went).

The second argument the Chinese government could make to explain its actions goes to the heart of the term *quarantine*. Beijing could say that it has been forced to respond to what the Taiwanese and the Americans are doing right now. Taiwan and the United States have announced various defense initiatives and arms sales. The two plan to bring many missiles and sensors to Taiwan, to reconfigure Taiwan's forces, and to deploy new weapon systems that, according to the Chinese government, are designed to menace Chinese defense forces and Chinese commerce.

So, in this scenario, the Chinese would say, "We see that Taiwan and these foreigners are preparing to send hundreds of missiles into Taiwan. We are not going to allow all these destabilizing and threatening weapons into our territory and we are going to run a quarantine to keep them out."

Any student of Cold War history will recognize that this scenario could seem analogous to the American position in the Cuban Missile Crisis of 1962. Instead of the United States quarantining Cuba to keep dangerous Soviet arms out of an island near the United States, the Chinese government would announce that it is quarantining Taiwan to keep destabilizing American arms and foreign military advisors, or other foreign military experts (civilian or military), out of its territory, as they see it, and Beijing could do this without occupying Taiwan directly, without necessarily blockading Taiwan by cutting off or even hindering oil or food supplies or passenger traffic, such as the daily ferries.

This scenario includes variations, in which China engages Taiwan's air and naval forces that contest this quarantine, or fires salvoes of missiles into Taiwan to intimidate its citizens into compliance. The point is that, in all of these scenarios, China neither invades Taiwan nor attempts to cut off supplies of food or energy, as it would in a full siege. The goal is to force Taiwan to accept a loss of control, cutting Taiwan off from, at least, transfers of military equipment and associated foreign experts.

This scenario places a heavy burden on foreigners to decide whether they will deliberately choose to make a military challenge to this assertion of Chinese sovereignty. In this context, with the Chinese making these arguments, the outsider, such as the United States or Japan, would first have to negotiate the divided and contentious domestic politics surrounding such a deliberate and dangerous military challenge. At the same time, all would be watching the behavior of Taiwan's citizens and their political divisions and quarrels about how to proceed.

Beyond the domestic political arguments, military officials could also argue about the feasibility of a military response. Chinese forces would have the advantage in numbers and logistical sustainment. Civilian shippers would likely do whatever the Chinese asked. If the United States wanted to fight its way in to make cargo deliveries of some kind, its military prospects would be problematical.

Another option for Washington and its allies and friends, however, would be to mount a counterblockade to interfere with shipping into China. They could take advantage of China's difficult maritime geography. In the last forty years, China has become a workshop to the world and its economy is now directed primarily toward the ocean, not inland toward the heartlands of Eurasia. This Chinese trade has various choke points, such as the Strait of Malacca between Malaysia and Indonesia, or the traffic through the Lombok and Makassar straits, passing through Indonesian islands.[122]

Yet the counterblockade response has severe problems of its own. It would be an escalation if the Chinese have only quarantined Taiwan, and not blockaded it. Such a quarantine might not be regarded, by many experts, as an act of war. The international law issue is whether Taiwan is part of China and, beyond that, the Chinese would not necessarily block vital supplies or commerce from going to and from Taiwan. The counterblockaders would be escalating toward war if they interfered with vital supplies or normal commerce to and from China. They would have to develop a list of the goods deemed to be contraband. These lists would have to be negotiated among any involved allied nations.

A second severe problem for a counterblockade option is that much of the trade involving East Asia actually occurs in the seas *inside* the first island chain. Regarding China, Taiwan, South Korea, and Japan, for all four economies, the other three tend to be their top trading partners. The commerce among those four societies is intense. Therefore, the counterblockader could have to extend the blockade to interfere with all that trade with all those negative consequences.

Third, the counterblockader would wonder whether even all this would quickly damage China in any serious economic way. China could still secure access to a great deal of its oil and gas through overland trade, above all from Russia, and, of course, the United States could not interdict China's borders with Russia.

Thus, an intrusive counterblockade against China would soon interfere with commerce that profoundly affected the economies of Japan, South Korea, and even Taiwan, among others. If Japan or South Korea actively supported a counterblockade, China could then attempt to blockade the sea lanes and the vital trade of those countries. Both are more vulnerable to such blockades than China. And Taiwan is the most vulnerable of them all.

This scenario could then seem to offer the prospect, to a Chinese planner, of relatively manageable risks and high rewards. China would not only demonstrate meaningful sovereignty; it would gain the military benefit of effectively blocking the further military modernization of Taiwan's defenses, possibly permanently. If that were successful, the longer-term effects on Taiwan's domestic politics could be imagined.

SCENARIO 3: CHINA INVADES TAIWAN

Chinese planners could consider an invasion of Taiwan in one of two ways. The first is the more traditional siege and amphibious assault, aided by an armada of ships and landings at some of a dozen or so beach areas on the northern and western sides of Taiwan, more or less facing the Taiwan Strait, all of them with prepared defenses.

A second approach (which could be combined with the first) would rely much more on airborne/heliborne assault and special operations. This approach is evocative of the German assault on Norway in April 1940, or especially the mainly airborne German attack on Crete in May 1941. In the assault on Crete, at no point did the Germans have complete control of the surrounding waters. But they did establish adequate control over the air above Crete, which allowed them to make life difficult for British naval vessels trying to operate in the area and to drop the troops that they needed, troops that were outnumbered by the defenders on the ground. Analysts could also look at the British air and sea attack on the Falkland Islands in the spring of 1982. This second approach could try to immediately decapitate Taiwan's government, occupy vital installations, and try to end the war quickly with that assault and by clearing the way for the landing of forces in less contested waves.

Military analysts stress, correctly, that in principle such assaults are risky and difficult operations. The Taiwanese would have some significant inherent advantages. The attacker could only get a small number of forces ashore in an initial assault. The defender should be able, if the defender were ready and determined, to amass much larger forces in the vicinity of the assault unless those forces can somehow be deflected and paralyzed by the attacker. And then the invader would need to sustain the forces that have made it ashore with the thousands of tons of supplies needed to maintain modern military operations.[123] Moreover, the weather in the Taiwan Strait can be challenging for complex operations most of the year. And Taiwan's terrain is not ideal for traditional amphibious assault.

Another big plus the Taiwanese would have, *in principle*, is that during the last ten years, missiles and sensors have been reaching such a high pitch of precision, at relatively low cost, that the defender armed with such weapons would enjoy some inherent advantages. If the defender had enough of these advanced missiles and enough survivable or relocatable sensors that could locate their targets, less expensive missiles could readily destroy large incoming targets such as ships and expensive aircraft.

This twenty-first-century conflict then becomes a new version of battlefields of World War I in which, for most of that war, if the defenses were settled, well armed, and well manned, they could create a no-man's-land. In the twenty-first-century case, that could apply to aircraft and surface vessels too. This is why knowledgeable former defense officials such as Michèle Flournoy and Bob Work have spoken publicly about the need to develop a capability to destroy every Chinese vessel in the South China Sea within seventy-two hours.[124] Also, there are many tiny islands and places where a defender could disperse small missile-firing groups of soldiers and Marines, as the U.S. Marine Corps commandant recently discussed. The Japanese Ryukyu chain offers a possible set of nearby mini-base locations.[125]

This could all be true, *in theory*. The first issue is then to analyze readiness and willpower of potential defending forces. Readiness includes the quantity of immediately available forces, including the inventories of the relevant missiles and sensors. No analyst in the public seems to believe that those quantities in Taiwan are currently even close to being adequate. Some write optimistically of five-year plans to attain more robust defenses.

There are other issues of readiness and willpower in the relevant armed forces. The Taiwanese forces have ended conscription and transitioned to an all-volunteer force. Their units appear to be undermanned, ill trained, and poorly equipped. These deficiencies are more notable in the nominally large reserve forces. Critics have pointed to a pattern of Taiwanese reliance on small numbers of expensive, more symbolic, aircraft and warships, good for political gestures, but not yet configured into the dispersed, highly capable twenty-first-century forces that could be postulated in theory. The U.S. forces in the region are not yet fully deployed there either; nor are the relevant Japanese forces.[126]

In early 2019, Taiwan's leaders announced a determined program to increase defense spending, emphasize innovative "asymmetric" defenses of the kind outside analysts have also been recommending, and build up domestic defense production for a more "self-reliant defense."[127] The former leader of Taiwan's military, Admiral Lee Hsi-ming, has been an important advocate of these dramatic improvements. "'How do you defend Taiwan? All I can hear is that the United States will intervene,' he said. 'What reason is there to believe that the United States will sacrifice the lives of its own children to defend Taiwan?' He added, 'My best bet is my own strength, to stop people from bullying me.'"[128]

Such a program will take years to reach fruition. As such a buildup begins in earnest, and evidence in the last year or two indicates that the wheels are starting to turn on both sides of the Pacific, the Chinese are also closely analyzing these developments.

What is happening, therefore, are dynamic cross-strait military developments that the Chinese are watching carefully and are to their disadvantage. Beijing then must argue internally about how to react during what they could judge to be a window of military advantage. This kind of window thinking was a marked aspect of the Cold War during its most dangerous phase, between 1949 and 1962.[129]

Another feature of the invasion scenario is that, even if the defenders were successful and the invasion turned into a prolonged siege, there is a question of how long a siege the defenders could withstand. How long could they actually hold out, for example, before they exhausted their inventories of missiles?

The operational objective, however, is not for Taiwan's military planners to defeat a prolonged and determined Chinese siege and eventual invasion. A realistic Taiwanese objective is to have forces that are visibly ready and willing to deter or defeat the fait accompli option of a rapid Chinese assault that overwhelms and decapitates the defenses before the Taiwanese can mobilize effectively and before others could choose to join the fight.[130] This defensive objective is theoretically attainable, especially if Taiwanese air defenses are decentralized and strong. We doubt that Taiwanese forces are currently adequate for this purpose.

The invasion scenario could appear, to a Chinese analyst, to have high risks but, from their perspective, lasting rewards that include a definitive resolution of the Taiwan sovereignty issue. The strategic question then is whether it is possible for Taiwan, the United States, and its allies to change that calculus about longer-term PRC gain.

A CREDIBLE
U.S. STRATEGY FOR
A TAIWAN CONFLICT

*PROPOSITION 1: DEFENSE STRATEGIES AND
CAMPAIGN PLANS*

We begin with the observation that defense strategies are campaign plans, in outline. If outsiders (or insiders) do not understand the likely campaign plan, they cannot comprehend the strategy. If outsiders (or insiders) cannot judge whether the campaign plan is credible, including the arrangements with allies and the sufficiency of forces, then there is no way to judge whether the strategy is credible.

A corollary to this proposition is that potential adversaries and allies should understand the campaign plan, in outline. That is not a mistake—if the goal is to prevent a war. During the central military confrontations of the Cold War, Washington and its allies had good insight into likely Soviet campaign plans, either for an attack on the United States or an invasion of Central and Western Europe. The Soviets and their allies had an excellent understanding of American nuclear war plans, in outline, and of NATO's campaign plans to defend Europe. Moscow gained this understanding not only from endless public discussion, but also from well-placed spies in NATO capitals and NATO headquarters. These mutual understandings helped deterrence to work. Movie fans will remember the famous scene in the movie *Dr. Strangelove*, in which the Soviet premier had to explain, with keen regret, that his government had developed a magnificent deterrent plan, their new Doomsday machine, but, unfortunately, he had not yet held the press conference at which he was going to tell the world about it. Thus, in that cinematic case, deterrence failed.

Our second observation is that, to have a credible campaign plan related to Taiwan, the planning needs to include participation and agreement by at least Taiwan and Japan. Officials can debate whether or how to include countries such as South Korea, or the Philippines, or Indonesia, or Malaysia, or Australia, or others. As we argue, an appropriate campaign plan is also very much political and economic, not just military.

The absolute minimum planning, though, would involve Taiwan and Japan. That coordinated campaign planning has to be done at a serious level and in a professional way, not with vague generalities. Those who are closer to that process than we are can judge how well that exacting standard is now being met. We are skeptical.

This observation about campaign planning is the surface expression of a deeper conviction: the United States cannot, and should not, care more about preserving Taiwan's democracy than the citizens of Taiwan—or the citizens of Japan. They are closest to the dangers. Those societies, in turn, will understandably be influenced by the attitudes of the United States. These societies will not think and act in lockstep. But their concerns and readiness must be in some fundamental alignment with the United States.

That is why the planning issues matter so much. The United States and Japan cannot credibly promise to behave automatically, robotically, regardless of the circumstances or Taiwan's actions. What they can credibly promise is to prepare to act. They can make those preparations plausible and visible. That process will, itself, help prepare their societies to act in a coordinated way.

A DIFFERENT KIND OF CAMPAIGN PLAN: A BERLIN SCENARIO

If the U.S. response to quarantine or invasion is for the U.S. military to fight its way through to rescue or liberate a besieged or embattled Taiwan, we do not see a credible conventional military solution by Washington in response to either. We do not think Taiwan, or the United States, or Japan should rely on a campaign plan that simply prolongs the fighting near Taiwan "long enough for U.S. forces to arrive on station to help repulse the assailants."[131] We do not believe the United States is able to sustain lasting sea and air warfare at the edge of the western Pacific, especially given that the available number of U.S.-flagged cargo ships has diminished and the existing ships are old and poorly maintained.

In the winter of 2017 to 2018, the Trump administration's National Security Council (NSC) staff approved a strategic framework that called on someone, apparently the United States, to "devise and implement a defense strategy capable of, but not limited to: (1) *denying* China sustained air and sea dominance inside the 'first island chain' in a conflict; (2) *defending* the first-island-chain nations, including Taiwan; and (3) *dominating* all domains outside the first island-chain." A further sentence was redacted from the document when the Trump White House declassified and released it in January 2021.

The document did not commit the United States to actually defend Taiwan. It called on the U.S. military to develop the capability to do so, in the quoted ways. Elsewhere the document stated the "objective," which we share, that the United States should "[e]nable Taiwan to develop an effective asymmetric defense strategy and capabilities that will help ensure its security, freedom from coercion, resilience, and ability to engage China on its own terms."[132]

Three years have passed since that guidance was secretly issued by the Trump NSC. We know of no credible expert who assesses that, in those last three years, as Chinese capabilities have advanced, U.S. defense strategy is now, on balance, more capable of performing the three quoted tasks. It is time, and past time, to devise a defense strategy to deal with the situation as it is, not as it could be sometime in the wishful future.

If missiles rule, Chinese missiles will keep the cavalry from riding to the rescue. As a pessimistic analyst put it, a more likely outcome of that scenario would be that "Washington is forced to capitulate after ideological twaddle comes crashing against the harsh and unforgiving rocks of reality in the form of the actual military balance of power (where it matters)."[133]

But this is not a new kind of strategic problem for the United States and its allies.

From 1945 to 1990, the United States, Britain, and France maintained military zones of occupation in West Berlin. West Berlin was entirely encircled by communist East Germany and by the hundreds of thousands of well-armed Soviet troops stationed in that country. If the Soviets decided to besiege or overrun West Berlin, the NATO allies had no conventional military solution to that problem. This became a real threat during two intense crises, a cutoff of land access in 1948 and 1949, and between 1958 and 1962 with a Soviet or East German threat to again end access (at a time when air supply was no longer an adequate solution), or even to overrun West Berlin.

The Allied strategy in both Berlin crises was a campaign plan in two parts. The first was to mount a carefully orchestrated military challenge to the denial of access sufficient to compel the Soviet government, or its East German ally, to use force and thereby initiate a war.

The second part entailed campaign plans that would rapidly escalate that local war into a general war, with likely first use of nuclear weapons by the United States in order to offset the expected imbalance of conventional forces. This was an extreme U.S. threat. Much of the tension in those years—especially between 1958 and 1962—arose from the challenges of how intense U.S. diplomacy could reassure allies that the threat was credible and demonstrate that credibility to the Soviet Union.[134]

A similar U.S.-Taiwan-Japan strategy for Taiwan would also have two parts. The first would be a carefully orchestrated military challenge of a PRC quarantine or of a siege and assault. Suppose, for instance, that the United States and Japan, in the roles that the United States and Britain played in the Berlin story, chose to prepare for such military contingencies. They would do so by planning to send a carefully designed multinational force, carrying supplies to Taiwan, to challenge the Chinese forces.

In the Berlin case, a U.S., British, and French military planning group called Live Oak worked, for years, on exactly how they would together conduct a possible military response to a denial of access to West Berlin. Separately, a diplomatic group that included the West Germans (the Quad) met regularly to plan coordinated policy on Berlin.

The coordinated military challenge would be calibrated to present Chinese forces with the choice to either let these neutral forces through or shoot down planes and sink ships, in a clash that would kill numbers of Americans or Japanese, or both. The Chinese would thus either initiate a local war (in the quarantine scenario) or widen it by choosing to attack these neutral vessels or aircraft.

For the quarantine scenario, and especially for the invasion scenario, the United States and allies, at least including Japan, should ready, and even preposition, stocks of relevant military equipment and other supplies that could help Taiwan defend itself, along with the means to ship them to Taiwan in a crisis or even during a Chinese assault on the island. A number of precedents are applicable. For example, both China and the Soviet Union sent military supplies (in the Chinese case, many troops) to North Vietnam throughout that country's war against South Vietnam and the United States. The Soviet Union shipped massive military supplies to Egypt and Syria during their 1973 war against Israel (as well as advisors to help assemble and repair equipment); the United States conducted a large military airlift of vital equipment to Israel as the war raged on.

A U.S. (or Japanese) decision to in fact make such a military challenge to a Chinese attempt to deny access would be momentous. It was a momentous choice in the Berlin crisis of 1948. It would have been an even more momentous choice in the second, more dangerous, Berlin crisis that lasted from 1958 through 1962. In the Taiwan case, a military challenge by the American and Japanese governments would put many lives at risk. Those governments would understand that this challenge could produce a larger conflict.

But in this Taiwan scenario, unlike the Berlin case, the second part of the U.S. and allied plan—if the Chinese attack their supplying forces and thus either triggered a local war or widened an ongoing war against Taiwan—would not be a U.S. and allied escalation to general war.

Instead, we propose a plan that would attempt to limit the fight to a local conflict over and around Taiwan. Taiwan may not end up winning that battle, in the short run, but its resistance could force China to face a much wider and lasting conflict. Instead of escalating to general war, this plan would prepare, in advance, the political and economic breaks and reactions that would likely accompany a local war with China, although the possibility of a wider war would still exist.

The trigger for this military, economic, and political conflict would be a local war over Taiwan in which Chinese forces killed Americans, and perhaps also Japanese and other allied forces or citizens. In this context, it is useful to recall and review what happens when the United States goes to war with a country, even a small war. First, the United States would freeze all assets owned by that country, or its citizens, in the United States. In this case, the United States could have to recognize an independent Taiwanese government, even in extremis a government-in-exile of some kind, in order to distinguish and protect Taiwanese-owned assets from being seized and possibly forfeited along with all Chinese-owned assets.

Second, the United States would cut off, and strictly control, any business transactions or dollar transactions with China. No trading with the enemy would be conducted. This would necessarily end any payment of interest on American securities, government or private, held by Chinese citizens or the Chinese government. It would include at least the suspension of interest payments on Treasury bonds held by the Chinese government or Chinese citizens.

These are profound measures. They would affect trillions of dollars of assets in the United States and around the world. We presume that China would retaliate in kind. These moves would immediately trigger a large and devastating financial and economic crisis (as also happened immediately after the outbreak of war in August 1914, because of the asset controls and commercial closures, not because of the impact of the military operations themselves).

These effects would be so great that it is not credible to threaten them as sanctions. We are not proposing a strategy of coercive diplomacy. This is a strategy to spell out how world politics and the world economy are likely to fracture after such a terrible break. That is why robust U.S. and allied local military capability is so essential. Without the impetus of an outbreak of fighting, Washington's deterrence threat of such gigantic measures could seem hollow.

However, if a violent local conflict does occur, such extraordinary measures would not only be adopted but also likely implemented practically overnight. If Japanese citizens had also been killed, and Japan was embroiled in the local war, then Japan would probably adopt a similar set of draconian measures.

This political-economic campaign plan should be prepared in advance with allies and paired with plans for a local military response to Chinese cross-strait aggression.

Next, there would also be a political-military campaign plan for the longer haul. This should not be one that assumes immediate escalation to a general war. If there is a real possibility of a local war over Taiwan in which China decided to violently establish its dominance over the island, fighting and killing Americans and perhaps Japanese and citizens of other nationalities in the process, both Japan and the United States should dramatically increase their military preparedness for such a conflict. What is needed, then, is a plan that would spell out, in advance, what the Americans, Japanese, and perhaps others would do in such a perilous situation. In this way, the likely U.S. and allied response should be considered, and comprehended, before the event, rather than waiting for events to unveil what in fact was foreseeable.

First, in the aftermath of a local war over Taiwan, Japan would probably move, immediately, to adopt a program of rapid rearmament and remilitarization. It would do so with strong American and other allied support. We believe Japan would regard a violent Chinese takeover of Taiwan as a threat to the vital interests of Japan, even its future independence and existence. Whether it is reasonable or not, we believe Japan would come to that conclusion. Many Japanese prefer peace and abhor the militarism of the past. But this could change. Outsiders should not underestimate just how fast and far Japanese society could move, and change, once a consensus has formed about the need to act. This part of the joint U.S.-Japan campaign plan should develop, in advance, the scale and character of how Japan should prepare to defend itself in the aftermath of a local war.

Second, a violent Chinese takeover that includes a local war in which Americans have fought and died would likely galvanize a buildup of American defenses on a scale not seen in more than a generation. This part of the campaign plan should develop, in advance, the scale and character of this buildup, to map out how a thoroughly roused United States would prepare to defend itself. In both cases, Japan and America—and possibly other states too—the plans would be credible precisely by being realistic about what would likely happen.

In sum, this overall campaign plan would be for a possible local military challenge that could well escalate into the rapid and disorderly division of the world into two economic spheres, within days or weeks, forcing countries and firms to make painful choices. Many opinion writers have mused about a Cold War 2.0 with China.[135] This series of events would produce such a global cold war (as the United States and its allies had kindred restrictions on Chinese and Soviet assets or transactions through much of the 1950s and 1960s).

The objective of this strategy is not to convince China that it should surrender. The objective is to develop a picture in Beijing of the world that could follow a local war over Taiwan. Although the United States and its friends would suffer painful sacrifices, China would have to redefine its future where it had provoked a division of the world in which a large part mobilized against China to an extent that had never happened before.

We believe that a credible strategy for a conflict over Taiwan is therefore not mainly about playing out scenarios for military escalation. Our alternative strategy does involve military escalation, but only to a point. These comprehensive plans emphasize the economic and political consequences of a deeply divided world. They invite Chinese leaders to consider as these U.S. and allied plans play out, would China—and the Chinese Communist Party—be better off than before they occurred? This, of course, is meant to be the essence of effective deterrence.

CONSIDERING THE STAKES: THE CZECHOSLOVAKIA CHOICE

To the historically minded, a Taiwan crisis could evoke the memory of the Czechoslovakia crisis of 1938. Taiwan is a democracy in a contested region facing revanchist claims by a neighbor that it is an artificial country. In 1938, Czechoslovakia was the last democracy left in Central and Eastern Europe. It was threatened with extinction by a Germany that asserted sovereignty over ethnic kinfolk, what the

Nazis called the German Volk, who lived in vital portions of Czechoslovak territory.

Historical analogies are pertinent for suggesting possibilities and questions. They are not useful in providing the answers to the questions. For the answers, one needs to look to the case at hand.[136] But thinking about the Czechoslovakia case does suggest some important similarities and differences.[137]

Czechoslovak citizens then, and Taiwan's citizens today, were and are divided about whether to resist and fight a powerful neighbor. On balance, the Czechs were readier and more willing to fight the Germans in 1938 than seems to be the case among Taiwanese today contemplating a possible war with China. Yet Taiwanese public attitudes as discussed earlier are evolving quickly in light of the events in recent years, so this is a moving picture.

In the 1938 crisis, what became crucial was the quality of coordination and joint planning between Britain and France. Today, Japan finds itself more in the role of France in 1938, which felt much closer to the conflict and had much greater affinity and responsibility to the new democracy in Prague. The French had a formal security agreement with Czechoslovakia. The British did not. But the British felt obliged to back the French.

Both the British and French were deeply divided, internally, about what to do. Their internal divisions transcended the English Channel as each side played in the other's domestic politics, as well as debated what to do in more traditional diplomacy. The quality of British and French coordination in 1938 left a lot to be desired and helped lead to war and continental defeat. We are not able to compare the quality of current U.S.-Japanese coordination over Taiwan if, for example, this crisis broke out in coming months, but we worry.

In 1938, the British and French reading of German politics and Hitler's immediate intentions was reasonably good. They were divided about what Hitler might do if he got his way on Czechoslovakia. Their understanding of German military capabilities was quite bad, however prone to exaggeration. This example should inspire due modesty now, along with closer questions about how well the United States, and its friends, understand either Chinese politics or Chinese military capability.

Above all, absolutely above all, the surpassing question prompted by reflections on the 1938 crisis is the great decision about when and where it is right to trigger a great conflict over a seemingly remote foreign struggle. Our proposed alternative strategy for Taiwan would posit a local military conflict that would trigger a catastrophically disruptive general political and economic conflict yet try to avoid or at least defer a general war. The great question for Americans and their allies to judge now is whether one of these Taiwan scenarios could be the road to a violent clash that could divide the world into fortresses, or worse.

As we argued earlier, we do not believe that decision can, should, or will be made in advance. No political leaders, either in the United States or Japan or elsewhere, will commit themselves to an automatic response that risks war. They should and will reserve such a decision until they have to make it. The particular circumstances at the time will matter, including, and not least, the behavior and stamina of the Taiwanese.

What we do recommend is that detailed plans should be made, in advance, that can give the leaders a more credible choice about what they could do in these scenarios than the plans currently evident to us. We also recommend that, if those plans are prepared, so too should be plans to conduct diplomacy that would seek to avoid this calamity and wind down the crisis.

Here again, in reflecting on diplomacy, the Berlin analogy is suggestive. After the Cuban Missile Crisis of October 1962, years of work followed to defuse tensions about the status of Berlin. Neither side abandoned its positions of principle. But a Quadripartite Agreement, signed in 1971, agreed on ways to reduce tensions and defer resolution of the underlying issues. The set of understandings about Berlin also included informal understandings about the scale of the Western military presence in Berlin.

SOME CRUCIAL ISSUES FOR FURTHER WORK

We briefly acknowledge some of the topics that, if ideas like ours gain traction, will warrant substantial further work. First, the Biden administration would need to decide how to devise a sustainable policy of arms sales to help defend Taiwan. We believe that the recent emphasis on asymmetric defensive systems is appropriate. It means the United States and other countries should continue to assist Taiwan to acquire the quantities of missiles and relocatable sensors, along with other defensive systems, that help deter various kinds of Chinese assaults from air or sea. We do not believe that U.S. forces should be deployed in Taiwan as military advisors.

Second, the United States, Japan, and possibly others should prepare the detailed orchestration of a possible U.S. and military response to a quarantine or siege, inspired by the Berlin-related Live

Oak precedent mentioned earlier. These rules of engagement will be difficult to devise.

In that phase, the American and allied naval forces would have to decide whether their surface ships are going to destroy all the Chinese surveillance assets, such as vessels from the maritime militia, that are within a line of sight of their units. If the warships were worried about Chinese preemptive strikes, they would have to consider destroying all the Chinese sensors tracking them with enough precision to enable targeting. They would also have to decide whether to use valuable weapons on those targets or save them for more dangerous possible targets given that it would be difficult for U.S. warships to replenish their inventories. The warships would have to make those decisions as soon as they believed the operations raised a significant danger of such Chinese strikes.

Also, the U.S. and allied forces would have to make decisions about whether to initiate anti-satellite operations, again, to avoid or reduce the quality of Chinese targeting. The Chinese would be looking at these choices as well. We do not believe that anti-satellite operations would be as urgent a necessity as nearby trackers, but this requires more expert study. Both sides would be using networks of sensors to track possible targets. We believe the United States should at least plan so that, in an initial stage, it would not have to target either satellites or sensors on the Chinese mainland. Both China and the United States would also be examining scenarios for escalation of their cyber operations.

As stressed, we recommend that the United States and its allies develop campaign plans that limit the geographic scope of their military operations. Unless the Chinese launch attacks on American or allied homelands, we believe it would be a grave mistake to plan on military operations that attack targets in mainland China. Such strikes should not be part of a military challenge to a Chinese quarantine or to a siege of Taiwan.

We are not suggesting that the United States should abandon the option to threaten such strikes in the event of a general war. But a campaign plan that relies on attacks on mainland China should also assume Chinese strikes into mainland Japan and the contiguous United States. Washington should develop a campaign plan that does not posit or rely on such a widened geographic scope.

Finally, we assume that, in any crisis of this kind, Russia, Iran, and North Korea would consider moves of their own to take advantage of the situation. It is also possible that any of these countries could support China more directly in a confrontation with the United States and its allies. We should be ready.

U.S. POLICY PRESCRIPTIONS

Earlier in this report, we discuss the security elements of U.S. policy toward Taiwan and propose a variety of policy prescriptions in that domain. Here we detail the diplomatic and economic actions that would take place alongside the security policy prescriptions.

1. *Consider how U.S. policy toward Taiwan affects U.S.-China relations.* Of course, the Biden administration should calculate in advance how any particular action on Taiwan is likely to affect relations between Washington and Beijing. This is only to say that much is possible to further develop U.S. ties with Taiwan, but limits are imposed by possible Chinese countermoves.[138] As John Locke wrote, "He that judges without informing himself to the utmost that he is capable, cannot acquit himself of judging amiss."[139] Given all that is at stake, this is no time for the United States to judge amiss regarding China and Taiwan.

2. *Examine how U.S.-China and U.S.-Taiwan policies affect other U.S. policy objectives.* Washington can use Beijing's cooperation on a variety of issues connected to U.S. vital national interests. The Biden administration will rejoin the Paris Agreement on climate, of which China—the largest polluter in the world—is a crucial member. To work with China on climate issues ought to be a Biden team priority, though many in Taiwan will worry that the United States will sacrifice Taiwan's equities to make progress on climate with Beijing. The same is true of collaboration with Beijing on virus and vaccine research, bounding North Korea's nuclear weapons and missile programs, and preventing Iran from acquiring nuclear weapons. In addition is the array of U.S.-China and international trade issues, which will have an important impact on the American economy and workers. All these central issues

of potential mutual benefit become more difficult if China and the United States become seriously crosswise on Taiwan.

3. *Adhere to the U.S. One China policy.* It is useful to again recall the exact wording of the profound compromise between Washington and Beijing in the 1972 Shanghai Communique that stabilized cross-strait relations for half a century: "The United States acknowledges that all Chinese on either side of the Taiwan Strait maintain there is but one China and that Taiwan is a part of China. The United States Government does not challenge that position."[140] Thus, for decades Washington has refused to say whether it believed Taiwan is part of China, or whether the Taiwanese should regard themselves as among the "Chinese" who maintain "that Taiwan is a part of China." The United States has therefore taken no position on sovereignty over Taiwan. Nevertheless, Secretary of State Pompeo opined on November 12, 2020, that "Taiwan has not been a part of China."[141] Read literally in the past tense, as a summary of the history, Pompeo's statement was false. For Washington to abandon the One China formulation, as he apparently recommends, would be a historic mistake and put the United States on an escalator to war with China. The Biden administration agrees as it demonstrated in its January 23 statement on U.S. policy toward Taiwan.

4. *Oppose any declaration of independence by Taiwan.* Taiwan is autonomous. Taiwan's leaders appear to understand, rightly, that this is no time for ostentatious declarations about Taiwan's legal status. As President George W. Bush stressed in 2003, "We oppose any unilateral decision by either China or Taiwan to change the status quo."[142] The old dual deterrence formula is the best that can be done for the foreseeable future—no declaration of independence by Taiwan, no use of force by China.[143]

5. *Maintain strategic ambiguity.* A current lively debate in the policy community centers on whether Washington should abandon its longtime ambiguous position regarding the use of military force in response to a Chinese attack on Taiwan. Note that the issue is not whether the United States would react strongly to a Chinese assault on Taiwan. Of course it would—with political denunciations, diplomatic offensives, economic sanctions, UN Security Council debates, and so forth. Washington would not ignore such naked PRC aggression, no matter how busy the day was along the Potomac.

First, the facts. The 1979 Taiwan Relations Act "directs the president to inform Congress promptly of any emerging threats, and for the two to determine together an appropriate response."[144] In 1982, President Ronald Reagan made Six Assurances to Taiwan, but none promised the use of U.S. force to defend Taiwan.[145] President George W. Bush in April 2001 said that the United States would do "whatever it took to help Taiwan defend herself" in the event of attack by China.[146] President Donald Trump in August 2020 stated that "China knows what I'm going to do," but declined to be more specific.[147] In none of these statements is an explicit U.S. commitment to use military force in a Taiwan crisis, a policy that goes by the phrase "strategic ambiguity."

In a recent article in *Foreign Affairs*, Richard N. Haass, president of the Council on Foreign Relations, and David Sacks of CFR argue that the United States should end strategic ambiguity and instead adopt "a policy of strategic clarity, making explicit that it would respond to any Chinese use of force against Taiwan." They have done a service in raising this important issue, but nothing in their "strategic clarity" formula would necessarily change in practice what the United States has said before on the subject.[148] Therefore, a U.S. declaratory policy of "strategic ambiguity" should remain unchanged.

6. *Intensify across the board consultations with China, consistent with Reagan's 1982 Six Assurances.* An energized U.S.-China discourse should be candid and high level—no rows of officials trading sermons across the table in Washington or Beijing. In restricted private exchanges, U.S. and Chinese leaders should systematically address how to avoid the long list of sharp policy differences producing enveloping confrontations in the bilateral relationship, including to create robust crisis management mechanisms between the two.

However, for an intensified high-level bilateral dialogue between Washington and Beijing to be fruitful, the United States should first clearly establish that it is enhancing its military, diplomatic, and economic power projection into the Asia-Pacific; intensifying interaction with allies, partners, and friends; and helping build up their economic and military strength. Nothing less will convince Beijing—which pursues classic realist policies based on the balance of power—that it has reasons, based on its national interests, to negotiate seriously with the United States to avoid worst-case outcomes.

7. *Reject regime change in China as a U.S. policy objective.* The Trump administration all but declared that it could not work with Beijing unless

the Chinese Communist Party no longer ruled China. As Secretary of State Pompeo repeatedly stressed, "Look, I reject the notion that we're living in an age of inevitability . . . that CCP supremacy is the future."[149] Quite apart from the abysmal record by the United States in attempting to foster regime change in other countries, as Philip Gordon convincingly demonstrates in a new book, this policy has no chance of success in the foreseeable future and obviously would end any possibility of arresting the sharply downward slope in U.S.-China relations.[150]

8. *Do not use U.S. policy toward Taiwan to bludgeon China or to weaken U.S.-China relations.* Curious as it may seem, some in the U.S. debate view policy toward Taiwan primarily as an instrument to accelerate the systemic decline of U.S.-China relations.[151] They appear to calculate that because China is enormously sensitive concerning the future of Taiwan, this is a perfect issue for Washington to provoke Beijing even though it would entail predictable dangerous consequences. This brings to mind Groucho Marx's threat to an intruder, putting his pistol to his own head and shouting, "One more step and I'll fire."

9. *Coordinate U.S. Taiwan policy bilaterally with Asian allies, especially with Japan; within the Quadrilateral Security Dialogue with Japan, Australia, and India; and with friendly governments in the region.* The United States cannot successfully compete with China, cannot pursue an effective policy toward Taiwan over the long term as a solitary actor, a unilateralist. Washington needs Asian and European allies, partners, and friends, beginning with Japan.[152] This will require:

- a U.S. recognition that these nations have great equities attached to the future of the U.S.-China relationship and its connection to the future of Taiwan;

- an acknowledgment that they do not wish to be forced to choose between their economic interests regarding China and their security underpinnings provided by the United States;

- an alteration in the U.S. approach from dominating nation to more accommodating interlocutor;

- more intense consultation with others before Washington makes decisions, especially with respect to China and Taiwan; and

- a greater U.S. willingness to take the national interests of allies into account.

It is striking in the current public debate regarding U.S. policy toward Taiwan how often the views of American allies on the subject are never mentioned. And it is unlikely that any U.S. ally will be enthusiastic about a substantial change in U.S. policy concerning Taiwan.

10. ***Regulate U.S. diplomatic interaction with Taiwan.*** Only cabinet officers for health policy, environment, and trade, as well as executive branch representatives at the undersecretary level and below, should visit Taiwan, and their Taiwanese counterparts should stop in the United States.

At the same time and given the usual multiplicity of voices, opinions, and policy prescriptions from Washington's main streets to its dark back alleys, the government of Taiwan should have no doubt about U.S. red lines regarding its behavior. Team Biden should speak with one voice concerning Taiwan and its relationship to the United States and China. As we have just seen with the Trump administration, that is hardly the norm in Washington, but especially in this case rigorous discipline is required.

11. ***Make a major new effort to enhance Taiwan's interactions with other governments and support Taiwan's position in international organizations that do not require statehood for membership.*** Washington should make use of its unique diplomatic reach to lobby countries, beginning with those in Europe, to strengthen their relationships with Taiwan. Given newfound European goodwill toward Taiwan and the negative effects of China's aggressive COVID-related diplomatic assaults on EU members, it is a propitious time to move ahead in that regard. Trilateral dialogues featuring U.S., European, and Taiwanese government officials, private-sector representatives, and public outreach would be a good step to forge ties and address new shared concerns about China.[153] The EU is the top source of foreign direct investment in Taiwan. Washington should encourage Brussels and Taipei to build on this foundation by signing an EU-Taiwan investment agreement that could reroute supply chains through U.S. partner economies, boost clean energy cooperation, and solidify economic links between like-minded states.[154]

Especially in the context of the coronavirus crisis, it is a travesty that Taiwan is not an observer at the WHO World Health Assembly. Despite efforts from the United States and Japan, China's objections mean Taiwan was not able to attend the November 2020 WHA.[155] It is outrageous that a densely populated and largely virus-free island of more than twenty-three million people would not have anything to contribute to the WHO. The organization's clumsy attempts to explain allegations of censoring references to Taiwan on its social media feeds only exacerbates charges that the WHO is unnecessarily antagonistic toward Taipei.[156] If Taiwan's accession is impossible because of China's economic power and influence with WHO members, the Biden administration should certainly include Taiwan in any ad hoc group to deal with the virus.

The International Criminal Police Organization (INTERPOL) is the world's largest police organization, 194 member states cooperating on law enforcement to make the world safer. Taiwan should be allowed to participate in the group. The internet-aided rise of transnational crime means that Taiwan's lack of access to INTERPOL resources hampers the island's ability to recognize threats within its borders, apprehend air passengers who use forged documents, and share information on suspected criminals at home.[157] INTERPOL would also provide a useful platform for states to tap into Taiwan's extensive experience combating cyberattacks and cross-border cybercrime.[158] The UN International Civil Aviation Organization also should welcome Taiwan's participation. Exclusion from the ICAO means that Taiwan cannot share its expertise with countries or offer information befitting its role as a regional air traffic hub. Lack of access to INTERPOL and ICAO resources is a danger not just to Taiwan, but also to any country accepting travelers from Taiwan. In addition, the United States should support an expanded role for Taiwan in non-UN agencies of which it is a member, such as the World Trade Organization, the Asia-Pacific Economic Cooperation, and an array of other standard-setting bodies.

Given China's coercive influence in these organizations, this will be an uphill U.S. effort. But Washington should keep up the pressure and never miss an opportunity to stress how counterproductive it is to exclude Taiwan from these groups.

12. **Promote Taiwan's democratic institutions and practices.** Despite a thriving economy and a democratic system capable of handling the challenges associated with the coronavirus pandemic, Taiwanese democracy is not an inevitability.[159] Taiwan's first presidential election did not take place until 1996, and its government still employs structures left over from nearly forty years of martial law. The Taiwan Travel Act, which encourages visits by U.S. and Taiwanese officials, passed

unanimously in both houses of Congress, and congressional representatives should do as they vote. The four major parties on both sides of the Pacific also have common ground on support for Taiwan's democracy in the face of China's coercive pressure.[160]

Exchanges should increase between the two judicial systems and law enforcement agencies. The Mutual Legal Assistance Agreement and cooperation on cross-border drug trafficking enforcement are a partial basis for such interactions.[161] If Taiwan continues to remain blocked from INTERPOL, intensified collaboration would improve security in both the United States and Taiwan and provide Taiwanese law enforcement with information it may not otherwise be able to access. The United States should also cooperate with Taiwan as part of a multilateral effort among open societies to combat disinformation through diplomatic and professional interaction and equip civil society to handle the challenges of an online information environment.[162]

Beyond federal agencies, ties between state government and through sister city links should multiply. Interactions at the most fundamental levels of government can bring the citizens and business communities of each society closer together and reinforce a robust U.S.-Taiwan relationship that extends beyond officials in Washington.

13. *Increase U.S. interaction with Taiwan's economy, especially in tech sectors and regarding global digital supply chains and standards.* The two economies took a significant step to this end when Taiwan Semiconductor Manufacturing Company announced a plan to build a $12 billion chip foundry in Arizona.[163] The new plant will produce semiconductor chips within American borders, secure supply chains, enhance security, and boost the high-tech economies of both the United States and Taiwan.[164]

The United States and Taiwan should build on this progress by collaborating on standards for emerging technologies, many of which largely rely on Taiwanese hardware. New rules for data privacy and cybersecurity could be underwritten by joint U.S.-Taiwanese capacities for innovation and high-end chip manufacturing so crucial to emerging technology sectors. If Taiwan can convince American companies of its commitment to security and privacy standards, the island will be an increasingly attractive destination for technology supply chains moving out of China.[165] Newly proposed U.S.-Taiwan talks to strengthen cooperation on semiconductors and other technologies and build a stronger front to combat Chinese coercion are a welcome effort to focus on economic collaboration between the two democracies.[166] Washington and

Taipei should establish a group of technology industry leaders, venture capitalists, and universities on both sides of the Pacific to aid Taiwan's effort to integrate its own hardware expertise with the software innovation the island lacks.[167] Initiatives such as the November 2020 memorandum of understanding on artificial intelligence (AI) and business signed by AI players in the United States, Taiwan, Indonesia, Japan, and Singapore, and the establishment of the U.S.-Taiwan Economic Prosperity Partnership Dialogue on 5G, secure supply chains, and other areas of interest should become more commonplace.[168]

14. **Conclude a bilateral trade agreement with Taiwan and integrate it into the Comprehensive and Progressive Agreement for Trans-Pacific Partnership (CPTPP).** In 2020, the United States traded more with Taiwan ($66 billion plus worth of imports and exports through September) than it did with India or France ($55.4 and $52.8 billion).[169] A Taiwan trade deal could help reroute supply chains from China to U.S. partners and provide both Taiwan and the United States with access to technology that can improve cyber capabilities and dual-use communication technologies.[170] Such an agreement should resolve U.S. concerns about Taiwan's lax intellectual property protections and restriction of American agricultural imports, and address Taiwanese displeasure with the Trump administration's steel and aluminum tariffs.[171]

A trade agreement could also lay the framework for similar deals between the United States and other like-minded partners and establish ground rules for emerging agenda items such as data privacy and cross-border data flows.[172] The House and Senate unanimously passed the TAIPEI Act, which calls for stronger U.S.-Taiwan bilateral trade; a bipartisan group of fifty U.S. senators encouraged the Trump administration to begin free trade negotiations with Taiwan; and Taiwanese President Tsai Ing-wen has stressed that a trade agreement with the United States was a top priority for her administration.[173]

Additionally, CPTPP member states should accept Taiwan's stated desire to join the group.[174] Taiwan's accession to the CPTPP would require it to make some of the trade liberalization reforms that the United States wants it to undertake.[175] China is applying leverage to CPTPP members such as Brunei, Malaysia, and Vietnam that have territorial disputes with Beijing, and adding Taiwan would increase the organization's strength and breadth.[176] It would also represent tangible progress toward the U.S. aim of integrating Taiwan into the Indo-Pacific economy.[177] However, the United States has limited influence to encourage Taiwan's accession to a group that Washington helped create and then abandoned, yet another reason for the United States to rejoin the CPTPP.

15. *Launch a major new joint initiative with Taiwan on health-care policy, especially regarding the coronavirus.* Taiwan has had the world's most effective response to COVID-19 and the United States would benefit from that expertise. In this context, Washington should do all it can to facilitate Taiwanese health assistance and advice beyond the WHO, as it did with the 2015 Ebola Prevention Training Center, which was run by American-trained professionals from Taiwan.[178] The United States and Taiwan should also make good on their August 2020 memorandum of understanding signed by the Taiwanese Ministry of Health and Welfare and the U.S. Department of Health and Human Services that promised joint training and cooperation on pandemic control, preventing drug misuse, and a $2 billion coronavirus program.[179]

Taiwan, with its robust medical manufacturing capacity and the technology to support it, would be a useful U.S. partner in the effort to shift medical supply chains away from China.[180] As the United States and the rest of the world realize the possibilities and limitations of an increasingly digital health-care environment, Taiwan's fluency in streamlining health-care data could help the American government better respond to the next global health emergency.[181]

16. *Encourage people-to-people exchanges between the United States and Taiwan.* Tourism should be encouraged between the two peoples. An increase in word-of-mouth accounts from Americans visiting Taiwan and vice versa could itself be an important aspect in improving cultural ties between the two societies.[182] University collaboration and faculty and student interaction should become the norm. More Taiwanese students should study in the United States, and more U.S. students should learn Mandarin and Asian politics in Taiwan, with increased scholarships and grants to initiatives like the Fulbright Program. In the 2018–19 academic year, 23,369 Taiwanese students studied in the United States. Only 1,270 American students matriculated in Taiwan compared to 11,639 who spent time in mainland China.[183]

Additionally, the United States should increase funding to bring Taiwan's citizens to the United States through programs such as the International Leadership Visitor Program, of which Presidents Ma Ying-jeou and Chen Shui-bian are graduates.[184] The respective medical professions should have regular exchanges. In March 2020, the United States and Taiwan made a promising step on that path by announcing their intention to collaborate on coronavirus tests, treatments, and vaccines; hold conferences with each other's experts; and share expertise—something that Taiwan has in abundance after its successful domestic campaign against the coronavirus.[185] Both societies should also intensify cultural interaction—including language, food, art, literature, and music. An increasingly difficult environment for nongovernmental organizations (NGOs) in China combined with Taiwan's stated desire to make the island friendlier to NGOs would help facilitate such exchanges.[186] The 2012 decision to include Taiwan passport holders in the U.S. Visa Waiver Program makes it much easier to promote U.S.-Taiwan people-to-people contacts among all sectors and levels of society.

17. **Consult closely with Congress on U.S. policy toward China and Taiwan.** Many members of the U.S. Congress form an anti-China engine. They issue only bills of indictment against the PRC but have no strategy to avoid conflagration. Given this unfortunate backdrop, the Biden team should mount an immediate effort to form a congressional constituency in favor of reversing the negative trends created by Trump and company concerning strategy toward China. At the same time, it should urge Congress to recognize the enormous regional and global stakes in the bilateral U.S.-China relationship and the need to avert worst-case outcomes, including vis-à-vis Taiwan.

18. **Discuss U.S. policy toward China and Taiwan with the American people.** China is increasingly unpopular with the vast majority of the American people. In the latest Pew poll, 73 percent had an unfavorable view of China. In particular, the U.S. public condemns what it regards as China's COVID-19 deceptions, its predatory economic policies, its aggressive foreign policies, and its violations of human rights.[187] This U.S. public perception can partially be explained by the unrelenting attacks on China by the Trump administration and the Congress, but neither has advanced a strategy for the United States to deal with Chinese power. That should be an early initiative by the Biden team, to begin with a presidential address to the nation that explains his objectives vis-à-vis China and how he intends to reach them. Serial denunciation of Beijing as conducted over the past several years by Washington is not a strategy; it also moves the United States briskly along the road to permanent and dangerous confrontation with China.

U.S. VITAL NATIONAL INTERESTS AND TAIWAN

We define U.S. vital national interest narrowly—"necessary to safe-guard and enhance Americans' survival in a free and secure nation." Vital is not the same as important. A vital interest is one for which the United States could properly order its citizens to go to war. In practice, such a vital national interest should be defined with great care. With respect to U.S. vital national interests and Taiwan, we earlier observed that the issue could depend on the surrounding circumstances, including Taiwanese behavior, Japanese views, our assessment of China's objectives, and the possibility of falling dominoes—or not.

The Czechoslovakia and West Berlin cases that we cite are so rich because they help illustrate how difficult these questions can be.

Was German subjugation or dismemberment of Czechoslovakia per se a threat to the vital national interests of Britain? The British government of Prime Minister Neville Chamberlain judged no. Was it a threat to the vital national interests of France? The French government of Édouard Daladier judged yes (though some of his ministers disagreed). Was a corollary threat of German subjugation of France a threat to the vital national interests of Britain? The Chamberlain government said yes. Hence, the dilemma.

Then, for Britain, was also the problem of the context. The issue was not just Czechoslovakia, but also the more brutal trend in Hitler's behavior in 1938, including his threat against the last democracy in Central and Eastern Europe. Czechoslovakia had a serious army and one of Europe's great arms industries, material that would help Germany if added to its capabilities. All this created the issue for Britain, as for France, of where to draw the line, if a wider conflict was coming.

To this day, knowledgeable historians argue about whether Britain and France should have gone to war against Germany in 1938 to protect

Czechoslovakia, or instead were right to use that crisis to delay profound decision, rearm more, and then count on public support for the security guarantee they made to Poland in the spring of 1939.

Was Soviet control of West Berlin per se a threat to the vital national interests of the United States, Britain, and France in 1948? Maybe not. The administration of Harry Truman (and the British and French governments) deferred that hardest choice through a massive airlift of supplies during the 1948–49 blockade of Berlin. The 1958 Berlin crisis was different. By then, the airlift path was no longer adequate. West Berlin had gained enormous symbolic importance to both sides, which saw it as central to the future of Germany and Western Europe. The administrations of Dwight Eisenhower and John Kennedy (and their NATO allies) believed that the defense of West Germany was a vital national interest, akin to the defense of their homeland.

To this day, knowledgeable historians argue about whether the United States, Britain, or France were right to threaten the onset of thermonuclear war if the Soviets and East Germans used force to deny allied access to West Berlin. The deterrent threat was so powerful, yet so terrifying that to make it raised awful dilemmas about how to demonstrate credibility.

Now to address the Taiwan case. Past episodes regarding the definition and application of vital national interests suggest how difficult these issues can be. They are not an unambiguous guide to how those questions should be answered today.

Our current conclusions concerning U.S. vital national interests and Taiwan are as follows:

1. Is a Chinese takeover of Taiwan per se a threat to U.S. vital national interests? No.

2. Would it be a threat to the vital national interests of Japan? Probably. The Japanese should answer this question—and share this assessment with their allies, beginning with the United States. In 1938, France had a treaty commitment to help defend Czechoslovakia. The Japanese have no such commitment to Taiwan and have not felt the need to adopt one.

3. Would a violent Chinese conquest or subjugation of Taiwan, unresisted by the United States, threaten U.S. vital interests? Perhaps, depending on assessments of China, Taiwan, Japan, and others, and not just on a reflexive incantation about American credibility.

4. Would the corollary threat of Chinese subjugation of Japan be a threat to the vital national interests of the United States? Yes.

5. Should the United States assume direct responsibility for the defense of Taiwan? No.

6. Should the United States help Taiwan defend itself? Yes.

7. Should the United States and Japan supply Taiwan in a crisis, confronting Chinese attempts to deny access and therefore, at a minimum, risk the outbreak of local fighting and loss of life? Perhaps. The United States, Japan, and others should credibly plan to be able to do this in order to have the choice; and in the crisis, they could well implement that plan, depending on the kinds of assessments we have mentioned.

8. If China attacks U.S. and Japanese resupplying forces and thereby widens the war, should the United States and Japan escalate to general war and mobilize to reconquer Taiwan? No.

9. But if China attacks U.S. and Japanese resupplying forces and thereby widens the war, should the United States and Japan freeze Chinese assets and mobilize for the heightened danger of general war? Yes.

All of these questions should be debated now rather than after a Taiwan crisis erupts.

CONCLUSION

The horrendous global consequences of a war between the United States and China, most likely over Taiwan, should preoccupy the Biden team, beginning with the president. It could be unlikely that a U.S.-China conflict would go nuclear and Beijing has repeated its no first use doctrine, but there is little doubt that China wants to grow its arsenal of a few hundred warheads and build a more sophisticated force that could employ hypersonic glide capabilities.[189] Millions of Americans could die in the first war in human history between two nuclear weapons states. A 2015 RAND Corporation study of the effects of U.S.-China combat determined that estimating military losses would be "exceedingly difficult." World War II, however, was the last time the United States lost a major warship, and one sunk vessel could turn into the deadliest U.S. military event since the Vietnam War.[190]

The outbreak of a great power war would likely produce a global recession, if not a depression. It would disrupt Asian and international trade, sever major supply chains, and could collapse international financial systems.[191] This would produce deeply painful economic consequences for U.S. allies, who trade more with China than they do with the United States. One study estimates that a single year of U.S.-China conflict could cause American GDP to decline by 5 to 10 percent.[192]

China could unleash cyberattacks on the United States. The New York Federal Reserve estimates that a major cyberattack on the U.S. financial system could cause 2.5 times daily GDP in forgone payments, and a Lloyd's of London and Cambridge University study predicted that a hypothetical blackout affecting fifteen states could cause $243 billion to $1 trillion in damages, as well as deaths resulting from disruption to health care, traffic, and industry.[193]

In 2013, hackers associated with the PLA reportedly tried to infiltrate companies that control U.S. critical infrastructure, including Telvent which provides remote access and holds blueprints to North and South American oil and gas pipelines.[194] In 2019, researchers uncovered a suspected Chinese plot to access American utility companies.[195] Additionally, in September 2020, a ransomware attack said to have originated in Russia hit U.S. hospitals during a coronavirus surge and forced doctors to switch to pen and paper record keeping and postpone certain medical procedures.[196] The outbreak of U.S.-PRC conflict could see multiple cyber events hit U.S. society and its allies in rapid succession.[197]

While Washington and Beijing were trading blows, Russia could threaten the Baltics, increase its presence in Ukraine, or provide oil and weapon support to China.[198] Iran would be unlikely to stand idle in the Middle East in such a crisis given U.S. attention directed elsewhere. Another factor is the allied dimension. In matters ranging from technology issues to criticism of China's handling of Hong Kong, U.S. allies have sometimes been hesitant to support Washington when American rhetoric and actions are deemed too provocative or come with high economic costs.[199] France and Germany refused to support the United States in the 2003 Gulf conflict. In a U.S.-China war, even Japan might not join the battle given its domestic politics and constitutional constraints and the United States could well fight alone, shattering its alliance system.

The horrific consequences for the United States and its allies of a conflict with China should remind all not to back Beijing against a wall on Taiwan. This brings us squarely back to what we propose should be the strategic objective of U.S. policy toward Taiwan—to preserve Taiwan's political and economic autonomy, its dynamism as a free society, and U.S.-allied deterrence—without triggering a Chinese attack on Taiwan.

That seems a sensible and balanced policy to us.

ENDNOTES

1. Stavridis in a conversation about the question, "Why Would China Not Invade Taiwan Now?" *Cipher Brief*, June 4, 2020, http://thecipherbrief.com/the-question-why-would-china-not-invade-taiwan-now.

2. See Graham Allison and Robert Blackwill, *America's National Interests* (Washington, DC: Commission on America's National Interests, 2000), http://belfercenter.org/files/amernatinter.pdf. This list may be contrasted with the terse list of "enduring vital interests of the United States" that the Trump administration's NSC staff prepared in the winter of 2017 to 2018, which, beyond "protect the homeland," simply stated truisms: "advance American prosperity; preserve peace through strength; and advance American influence." NSC, "U.S. Strategic Framework for the Indo-Pacific," undated but prepared in the winter of 2017–18 by Matthew Pottinger for then National Security Adviser H.R. McMaster and released in January 2021 by National Security Adviser Robert O'Brien, http://trumpwhitehouse.archives.gov/wp-content/uploads/2021/01/IPS-Final-Declass.pdf.

3. Taiwan beginning in the 1960s did have an active nuclear program, but shut it down in 1988 under American pressure. Kyle Mizokami, "China's Greatest Nightmare: Taiwan Armed with Nuclear Weapons," *National Interest*, September 12, 2019, http://nationalinterest.org/blog/buzz/chinas-greatest-nightmare-taiwan-armed-nuclear-weapons-80041.

4. See, on the issue of identity in a less inflamed and more economic context several years ago, Syaru Shirley Lin, *Taiwan's China Dilemma: Contested Identities and Multiple Interests in Taiwan's Cross-Strait Economic Policy* (Stanford, CA: Stanford University Press, 2016).

5. See Michael Mazza, "Why Defending Taiwan Is an American Political Consensus," *Global Taiwan Brief*, November 4, 2020, http://globaltaiwan.org/2020/11/vol-5-issue-21/#MichaelMazza11042020; Kenji Minemura, "Interview/ John Mearsheimer: U.S.-China Rift Runs Real Risk of Escalating Into a Nuclear War," *Asahi Shimbun*, August 17, 2020, http://asahi.com/ajw/articles/13629071; Brian Stewart, "Defend Taiwan Now, or Lose it Forever," *Bulwark*, June 24, 2020, http://thebulwark.com/defend-taiwan-now-or-lose-it-forever; and Ray Dalio, "Chapter 7: US-China Relations and Wars," *Principled Perspectives* (blog), September 25, 2020, http://linkedin.com/pulse/chapter-7-us-china-relations-wars-ray-dalio.

6. Regarding how Joe Biden would act if China crossed a "red line" between it and Taiwan, Japanese State Minister of Defense Yasuhide Nakayama said, "The United States is the leader of the democratic countries. I have a strong feeling to say: America, be strong!" Ju-min Park, "Japan Official, Calling Taiwan 'Red Line,' Urges Biden to 'Be Strong,'" Reuters, December 25, 2020, http://reuters.com/article/us-japan-usa-taiwan-china-idUSKBN28Z0JR; see also Patrick Winn, "Japan Has Plutonium, Rockets and Rivals. Will It Ever Build a Nuke?" *Public Radio International*, March 14, 2019, http://interactive.pri.org/2019/03/japan-nuclear/index.html.

7. For domino theory arguments applied to Taiwan, see Hal Brands, "China's Rise Heralds Return of the Domino Theory," Bloomberg, June 26, 2020, http://bloomberg.com/opinion/articles/2020-06-27/korean-war-anniversary-china-and-return-of-the-domino-theory; and Yi-Zheng Lian, "Will Taiwan Be the First Domino to Fall to China?," *New York Times*, November 27, 2018, http://nytimes.com/2018/11/27/opinion/taiwan-election-china-interference-domino-theory.html. For a succinct history of the domino theory's influence on U.S. foreign policy in the twentieth century, see Sam Tanenhaus, "The World: From Vietnam to Iraq; The Rise and Fall and Rise of the Domino Theory," *New York Times*, March 23, 2003, http://nytimes.com/2003/03/23/weekinreview/the-world-from-vietnam-to-iraq-the-rise-and-fall-and-rise-of-the-domino-theory.html.

8. See Cheng Li, "Hopes and Doubts in Beijing: Resetting U.S.-Chinese Relations Won't Be Easy," *Foreign Affairs*, November 13, 2020, http://foreignaffairs.com/articles/united-states/2020-11-13/hopes-and-doubts-beijing.

9. For an earlier and much briefer enumeration of these principles, see Robert D. Blackwill, "Nine Theses on U.S.-China Relations," *National Interest*, August 11, 2020, http://nationalinterest.org/feature/nine-theses-us-china-relations-166673. For a short assessment of the challenges of U.S.-China strategic competition, see Jeffrey Bader, "Meeting the China Challenge: A Strategic Competitor, Not an Enemy," in *The Future of US Policy Toward China: Recommendations for the Biden Administration*, edited by Ryan Hass, Ryan McElveen, and Robert D. William (Washington, DC: Brookings Institution and Yale Law School, 2020), 1–6, http://brookings.edu/wp-content/uploads/2020/11/Future-U.S.-policy-toward-China-v8.pdf.

10. See Ely Ratner, Daniel Kliman, Susanna V. Blume, Rush Doshi, et al., *Rising to the China Challenge: Renewing American Competitiveness in the Indo-Pacific* (Washington, DC: Center for a New American Security, 2019), http://s3.us-east-1.amazonaws.com /files.cnas.org/documents/CNAS-Report-NDAA-final-6.pdf; Oriana Skylar Mastro, "The Stealth Superpower: How China Hid Its Global Ambitions," *Foreign Affairs*, January/February 2019, http://foreignaffairs.com/articles/china/china-plan-rule-asia; and White House, "National Security Strategy of the United States of America," December 2017, 25, http://hsdl.org/?abstract&did=806478.

11. For PRC views of American decline, see Julian Gewirtz, "China Thinks America Is Losing: Washington Must Show Beijing It's Wrong," *Foreign Affairs*, November/ December 2020, http://foreignaffairs.com/articles/united-states/2020-10-13/china -thinks-america-losing. For an assessment of Beijing's strategy to drive a wedge between U.S. allies, see Lily Kuo, "'Divide and Conquer': China Puts the Pressure on US Allies," *Guardian*, February 2, 2019, http://theguardian.com/world/2019/feb/02 /divide-and-conquer-china-puts-the-pressure-on-us-allies; Tao Peng, "China's Plan to Break Off US Allies," *Diplomat*, January 19, 2019, http://thediplomat.com/2019/01 /chinas-plan-to-break-off-us-allies; and Thomas Wright and Thorsten Benner, "China's Relations with U.S. Allies and Partners in Europe," Brookings Institution, April 5, 2018, http://brookings.edu/testimonies/chinas-relations-with-u-s-allies-and -partners-in-europe.

12. Lee Kuan Yew, quoted in Graham Allison and Robert D. Blackwill, *Lee Kuan Yew: The Grand Master's Insights on China, the United States, and the World* (Cambridge, MA: MIT Press, 2013), 2.

13. Lee Kuan Yew, "China's Growing Might and the Consequences," *Forbes*, March 28, 2011; see also Hal Brands, "China Is Determined to Reshape the Globe," Bloomberg, October 29, 2019, http://bloomberg.com/opinion/articles/2019-10-30/china-is -determined-to-reshape-the-globe.

14. Following President Trump's September 2020 UN speech lashing out at China's COVID-19 response and touting his America First view, Xi delivered a speech that closed with "Let us join hands to uphold the values of peace, development, equity, justice, democracy and freedom shared by all of us and build a new type of international relations and a community with a shared future for mankind." Donald J. Trump, "Remarks by President Trump to the 75th Session of the United Nations General Assembly" (speech, Washington, DC, September 22, 2020), http:// mr.usembassy.gov/remarks-by-president-trump-to-the-75th-session-of-the-united -nations-general-assembly/; and Xi Jinping, "Speech at the General Debate of the 75th Session of the United Nations General Assembly" (speech, Beijing, September 23, 2020), http://news.cgtn.com/news/2020-09-23/Full-text-Xi-Jinping-s-speech-at -General-Debate-of-UNGA-U07X2dn8Ag/index.html. See also Sarah Zheng, "Time for a Reset in US-China Relations, Foreign Minister Wang Yi Says," *South China Morning Post*, December 7, 2020, http://scmp.com/news/china/diplomacy/article /3112842/time-reset-us-china-relations-says-foreign-minister-wang-yi.

15. See Andreas B. Forsby, "What Is Behind China's Diplomacy of Indignation?," *Diplomat*, November 13, 2020, http://thediplomat.com/2020/11/what-is-behind -chinas-diplomacy-of-indignation.

16. Beijing's seizure of a port in Hambantota, Sri Lanka, is a well-known example of poor outcomes for BRI countries, but Pakistan, Djibouti, the Maldives, and at least five other nations face the risk of debt distress as a result of BRI projects. John Hurley, Scott Morris, and Gailyn Portelance, *Examining the Debt Implications of the Belt and Road Initiative from a Policy Perspective* (Washington, DC: Center for Global Development, 2018), 11, http://cgdev.org/sites/default/files/examining-debt-implications-belt-and-road-initiative-policy-perspective.pdf.

17. See Harsh V. Pant, "For Beijing and New Delhi, 2020 Was the Point of No Return," *Foreign Policy*, December 28, 2020, http://foreignpolicy.com/2020/12/28/for-beijing-and-new-delhi-2020-was-the-point-of-no-return; Ajai Shukla, "How China and India Came to Lethal Blows," *New York Times*, June 19, 2020, http://nytimes.com/2020/06/19/opinion/China-India-conflict.html; Alastair Gale and Rajesh Roy, "U.S., Japan, India and Australia Strengthen Ties to Counter China," *Wall Street Journal*, October 6, 2020, http://wsj.com/articles/u-s-japan-india-and-australia-strengthen-ties-to-counter-china-11601986397; Anik Joshi, "China Is Pushing India Closer to the United States," *Foreign Policy*, June 9, 2020, http://foreignpolicy.com/2020/06/09/china-india-border-united-states-pakistan; and Pranshu Verma, "In Wake of Recent India-China Conflict, U.S. Sees Opportunity," *New York Times*, October 3, 2020, http://nytimes.com/2020/10/03/world/asia/india-china-trump.html.

18. World Bank, "GDP (current US$) - United States, Japan, Korea, Rep., Australia, China," accessed October 22, 2020, http://data.worldbank.org/indicator/NY.GDP.MKTP.CD?end=2019&locations=US-JP-KR-AU-CN&start=2019&view=bar; and "GDP, PPP (Current International $) - United States, Japan, Korea, Rep., Australia, China," World Bank, accessed November 16, 2020, http://data.worldbank.org/indicator/NY.GDP.MKTP.PP.CD?contextual=default&end=2019&locations=US-JP-KR-AU-CN&start=2019&view=bar.

19. World Bank, "Exports of Goods and Services (current US$)," accessed October 22, 2020, http://data.worldbank.org/indicator/NE.EXP.GNFS.CD.

20. Mark Cancian, "The High Times May Be Ending for U.S. Defense Spending," *Forbes*, October 4, 2020, http://forbes.com/sites/markcancian/2018/10/04/industry-should-hedge-its-bets-on-the-defense-budget/#27cf876c3965; "Chapter Two: Comparative Defence Statistics," *Military Balance* 120 (2020): 21, http://tandfonline.com/doi/pdf/10.1080/04597222.2020.1707962; Frederico Bartels, "China's Defense Spending Is Larger Than It Looks," Defense One, March 25, 2020, http://defenseone.com/ideas/2020/03/chinas-defense-spending-larger-it-looks/164060; and "Chapter Six: Asia," *Military Balance* 119 (2019): 222, http://tandfonline.com/doi/pdf/10.1080/04597222.2018.1561032.

21. For an assessment, see Michael E. O'Hanlon, "What the Pentagon's New Report on China Means for US Strategy — Including on Taiwan," Brookings Institution, September 4, 2020, http://brookings.edu/blog/order-from-chaos/2020/09/04/what-the-pentagons-new-report-on-china-means-for-u-s-strategy-including-on-taiwan.

22. See Yaroslav Trofimov, Drew Hinshaw, and Kate O'Keeffe, "How China Is Taking Over International Organizations, One Vote at a Time," *Wall Street Journal*, September 29, 2020, http://wsj.com/articles/how-china-is-taking-over-international-organizations-one-vote-at-a-time-11601397208; and United Nations, "Executive Heads," Chief Executives Board for Coordination, accessed October 22, 2020, http://unsystem.org/content/executive-heads.

23. See also Vladimir Isachenkov, "Putin: Russia-China Military Alliance Can't Be Ruled Out," Associated Press, October 22, 2020, http://apnews.com/article/beijing-moscow -foreign-policy-russia-vladimir-putin-1d4b112d2fe8cb66192c5225f4d614c4.

24. See Steven Lee Myers, "With Concessions and Deals, China's Leader Tries to Box Out Biden," *New York Times*, January 3, 2021, http://nytimes.com/2021/01/03/world/asia /china-eu-investment-biden.html; and European Commission, "EU and China reach agreement in principle on investment," Press release, December 30, 2020, http:// ec.europa.eu/commission/presscorner/detail/en/IP_20_2541.

25. China maintains a lead over the United States in 5G technology, but the United States is considered ahead in artificial intelligence, quantum computing, and semiconductors. For assessments of U.S.-China technology competition, see "America Still Leads in Technol- ogy, But China Is Catching Up Fast," *Economist*, May 16, 2019, http://economist.com /special-report/2019/05/16/america-still-leads-in-technology-but-china-is-catching -up-fast; Audrey Cher, "'Superpower Marathon': U.S. May Lead China in Tech Right Now — But Beijing Has the Strength to Catch Up," CNBC, May 17, 2020, http://cnbc .com/2020/05/18/us-china-tech-race-beijing-has-strength-to-catch-up-with-us-lead .html; and Asa Fitch and Stu Woo, "The U.S. vs. China: Who Is Winning the Key Tech- nology Battles?," *Wall Street Journal*, April 12, 2020, http://wsj.com/articles/the-u-s-vs -china-who-is-winning-the-key-technology-battles-11586548597.

26. In a 2020 Pew poll of fourteen developed countries in Europe, Asia, and North America, a majority in all countries had an unfavorable view of China. Belgium, where an equal amount have a favorable view of China or the United States, was the only one in which a majority did not see the United States as more favorable than China. In a survey released in the summer of 2020, a plurality of Germans and a majority of French, British, and Americans viewed China as a "force for bad in the world." Laura Silver, Kat Devlin, and Christine Huang, *Unfavorable Views of China Reach Historic Highs in Many Countries*, Pew Research Center, October 6, 2020, http://pewresearch .org/global/2020/10/06/unfavorable-views-of-china-reach-historic-highs-in-many -countries; "Negative Views of Both U.S. and China Abound Across Advanced Economies Amid COVID-19," Pew Research Center, October 6, 2020, http:// pewresearch.org/fact-tank/2020/10/06/negative-views-of-both-us-and-china-amid -covid-19; and "China's Role in the World," Tony Blair Institute for Global Change, June 2020, http://institute.global/sites/default/files/2020-06/Tony%20Blair%20 Institute%2C%20China%27s%20Role%20in%20the%20World.pdf. See also *European Public Opinion on China in the Age of COVID-19* (Olomouc, Czech Republic: Palacky University Olomouc, 2020), http://ifri.org/sites/default/files/atoms/files /european_public_opinion_on_china_in_the_age_of_covid-19.pdf.

27. See David Von Drehle, "China Has Lost Its Confidence," *Washington Post*, December 4, 2020, http://washingtonpost.com/opinions/global-opinions/china-has-lost-its -confidence/2020/12/04/2f1171b8-364f-11eb-b59c-adb7153d10c2_story.html; Philip Citowicki, "Domestic Vulnerabilities Lie Behind China's Aggressive Expansion," *Interpreter* (blog), February 14, 2020, http://lowyinstitute.org/the-interpreter/domestic -vulnerabilities-lie-behind-china-s-aggressive-expansion; Steven Lee Myers, Jin Wu, and Claire Fu, "China's Looming Crisis: A Shrinking Population," *New York Times*, January 17, 2020, http://nytimes.com/interactive/2019/01/17/world/asia/china-population -crisis.html; and Joseph S. Nye, "Commentary: China a Country With Great Strengths,

but Also Important Weaknesses," Channel News Asia, April 12, 2019, http://
channelnewsasia.com/news/commentary/china-us-rivalry-cooperation-strengths
-weaknesses-11424970.

28. Trump and Xi did not speak after March 2020, and since 2017 the Trump administration canceled nearly one hundred exchange forums with Beijing, including sixteen Joint Commission on Commerce and Trade working groups (David Nakamura, "Trump Promised to Bring China to Heel. He Didn't and the Result Is a Pitched Conflict Between the World's Two Major Powers," *Washington Post*, October 11, 2020, http://
washingtonpost.com/politics/trump-china-xi-biden/2020/10/11/9c6e3146-0270-11eb
-a2db-417cddf4816a_story.html; and Christopher Anstey and Peter Martin, "Trump-Xi Rift Plays Out With Some 100 Canceled Exchanges, Talks," Bloomberg, September 4, 2020, http://bloomberg.com/news/articles/2020-09-04/trump-xi-rift-plays-out-with
-some-100-canceled-exchanges-talks).

29. For a range of arguments advocating a U.S.-China grand bargain, see Andy Zelleke, "What Is the End Game of US-China Competition?," *Diplomat*, November 3, 2020, http://thediplomat.com/2020/11/what-is-the-end-game-of-us-china-competition; Kevin Lu, "The Pieces Are in Place for a Grand Bargain With China," *Foreign Policy*, November 28, 2018, http://foreignpolicy.com/2018/11/28/the-pieces-are-in-place-for
-a-grand-bargain-with-china; Matthew P. Goodman, "A Grand Bargain to Strengthen the Global Economic Order," in *Parallel Perspectives on the Global Economic Order: A U.S.-China Essay Collection*, edited by Daniel Remler and Ye Yu (Washington, DC: Center for Strategic and International Studies, 2017), http://csis-website-prod
.s3.amazonaws.com/s3fs-public/publication/170922_Remler_ParallelPerspectives
_Web.pdf; and Charles L. Glaser, "A U.S.-China Grand Bargain? The Hard Choice Between Military Competition and Accommodation," *International Security* 39, no. 4 (2015), 49–50, http://mitpressjournals.org/doi/abs/10.1162/ISEC_a_00199#
.WLidXVXyuUk.

30. Mutual Defense Treaty Between the United States and the Republic of China, December 2, 1954, 6 UST 433.

31. Richard M. Nixon, "Asia After Viet Nam," *Foreign Affairs*, October 1967, http://
foreignaffairs.com/articles/united-states/1967-10-01/asia-after-viet-nam.

32. U.S. Department of State, *Foreign Relations of the United States: China, 1969–1972*, edited by Daniel J. Lawler and Erin R. Mahan (Washington: Government Printing Office, 2010), Document 136, 350, http://history.state.gov/historicaldocuments
/frus1969-76v17/d136.

33. Richard M. Nixon, "President Nixon Announces Trip to China" (speech, Burbank, CA, July 15, 1971), http://china.usc.edu/richard-nixon-announces-he-will-visit-china
-july-15-1971.

34. U.S. Department of State, *Foreign Relations of the United States*, Document 203, http://
history.state.gov/historicaldocuments/frus1969-76v17/d203.

35. The United States and the People's Republic of China (U.S. and PRC), "Joint Communique of the United States of America and the People's Republic of China," January 1, 1979, http://ait.org.tw/our-relationship/policy-history/key-u-s-foreign-policy-documents
-region/u-s-prc-joint-communique-1979.

36. *Hearing on the Taiwan Relations Act, Before the House International Relations Comm.*,
     108th Cong. 2 (2004) (Statement of Richard Bush, Brookings Institution), http://
     brookings.edu/wp-content/uploads/2016/06/bush20040421-1.pdf; and Dennis
     Van Vranken Hickey, "The Taiwan Relations Act: A Mid-Life Crisis at 35?" Wilson
     Center, March 2014, 2, http://wilsoncenter.org/sites/default/files/media/documents
     /publication/TRAPolicyBrief.Hickey.pdf.

37. Taiwan Relations Act of 1979, Pub. L. No. 98-6, 22 Stat. 14 (3301).

38. U.S. and PRC, "U.S.-PRC Joint Communique," August 17, 1982, http://ait.org.tw/our
     -relationship/policy-history/key-u-s-foreign-policy-documents-region/u-s-prc-joint
     -communique-1982.

39. Lawrence Eagleburger to James Lilley, "Taiwan Arms Sales," cable, July 10, 1982,
     http://ait.org.tw/our-relationship/policy-history/key-u-s-foreign-policy-documents
     -region/six-assurances-1982.

40. George Shultz to James Lilley, "Taiwan Arms Sales," cable, August 17, 1982, http://
     ait.org.tw/our-relationship/policy-history/key-u-s-foreign-policy-documents-region
     /six-assurances-1982.

41. Annabel Virella, "20 Years Later: Reevaluating the Taiwan Policy Review," Project
     2049 Institute, April 3, 2017, http://project2049.net/2017/04/03/20-years-later
     -reevaluating-the-taiwan-policy-review; *Hearing of the East Asian And Pacific Affairs
     Subcomm. of the Senate Foreign Relations Comm.*, 103rd Cong. (1994) (Statement of
     Winston Lord, Assistant Secretary of State for East Asian and Pacific Affairs), 13, 15,
     http://eapasi.com/uploads/5/5/8/6/55860615/appendix_75_--_us_taiwan_policy
     _review_ii__1994_.pdf; and Richard C. Bush, *A One-China Policy Primer*, Brookings
     Institution, March 2017, 16, http://brookings.edu/wp-content/uploads/2017/03/one
     -china-policy-primer.pdf.

42. Steven Greenhouse, "Clinton Rebuffs Senate on Letting Taiwan President Visit U.S.,"
     New York Times, May 11, 1995, http://nytimes.com/1995/05/11/world/clinton-rebuffs
     -senate-on-letting-taiwan-president-visit-us.html; and Bush, *A One-China Policy
     Primer*, 15.

43. Warren Christopher, "American Interests and the U.S. China Relationship" (speech,
     New York, May 17, 1996), 3, http://eapasi.com/uploads/5/5/8/6/55860615/96-05-17
     _speech-_american_interests_and_the_u.s._china_relationship.pdf.

44. John M. Broder, "Clinton in China: The Overview; Clinton Tells of Hopes and Risks on
     Trade," *New York Times*, July 1, 1998, http://nytimes.com/1998/07/01/world/clinton
     -in-china-the-overview-clinton-tells-of-hopes-and-risks-on-trade.html.

45. We thank Raymond Burghardt for this important observation.

46. Bush, *A One-China Policy Primer*, 14; and Alex Frew McMillan and Reuters, "Taiwan
     Enters WTO With Eye on China," CNN, January 1, 2002, http://edition.cnn.com/2002
     /BUSINESS/asia/01/01/taiwan.wtoofficial/index.html.

47. American Presidency Project, "The President's News Conference with President
     Jiang Zemin of China in Crawford, Texas," October 25, 2002, http://presidency.ucsb
     .edu/documents/the-presidents-news-conference-with-president-jiang-zemin-china
     -crawford-texas.

48. Brian Knowlton, "Bush Warns Taiwan to Keep Status Quo: China Welcomes U.S. Stance," *International Herald Tribune*, December 10, 2003, http://nytimes.com/2003 /12/10/news/bush-warns-taiwan-to-keep-status-quo-china-welcomes-us-stance.html.

49. Anti-Secession Law of the People's Republic of China (2005), Embassy of the People's Republic of China, http://china-embassy.org/eng/zt/999999999/t187406.htm; and George W. Bush, interview by Neil Cavuto, *Your World With Neil Cavuto*, June 8, 2005, http://foxnews.com/transcript/transcript-president-bush-on-your-world.

50. Mark Landler, "No New F-16's for Taiwan, but U.S. to Upgrade Fleet," *New York Times*, September 18, 2011, http://nytimes.com/2011/09/19/world/asia/us-decides -against-selling-f-16s-to-taiwan.html.

51. Marc A. Thiessen, "Donald Trump Is the Most Pro-Taiwan President in U.S. History," *Washington Post*, January 14, 2020, http://washingtonpost.com/opinions/2020/01/14 /donald-trump-is-most-pro-taiwan-president-us-history; "Visa Waiver Program," American Institute in Taiwan, accessed January 5, 2020, http://ait.org.tw/visas/visa -waiver-program; Ankit Panda, "US Finalizes Sale of *Perry*-Class Frigates to Taiwan," *Diplomat*, December 20, 2014, http://thediplomat.com/2014/12/us-finalizes-sale-of -perry-class-frigates-to-taiwan; and Bush, *A One-China Policy Primer*, 17.

52. Bonnie S. Glaser and Michael J. Green, "What Is the U.S. 'One China' Policy, and Why Does it Matter?," Center for Strategic and International Studies, January 3, 2017, http://csis.org/analysis/what-us-one-china-policy-and-why-does-it-matter.

53. Roberta Rampton and Jeff Mason, "Obama Says China Would Not Take Change in U.S. Policy on Taiwan Lightly," Reuters, December 16, 2016, http://reuters.com/article/us -usa-obama-china/obama-says-china-would-not-take-change-in-u-s-policy-on-taiwan -lightly-idUSKBN1452PL.

54. See Thiessen, "Donald Trump Is the Most Pro-Taiwan."

55. Brad Lendon, "US Finalizes Sale of 66 F-16 Fighters to Taiwan as China Tensions Escalate," CNN, August 17, 2020, http://cnn.com/2020/08/17/asia/taiwan-us-f-16 -fighter-purchase-intl-hnk-scli/index.html.

56. Nick Aspinwall, "Taiwan President to Stop in Denver as US-Taiwan Ties Strengthen," *Diplomat*, July 19, 2019, http://thediplomat.com/2019/07/taiwan-president-to-stop -in-denver-as-us-taiwan-ties-strengthen; and Amy Qin, "As U.S. and Taiwan Celebrate a Bond, China Responds With Screaming Jets," *New York Times*, August 9, 2020, http://nytimes.com/2020/08/09/world/asia/taiwan-us-azar-china.html.

57. Amy Qin, "U.S. Official Visits Taiwan, and China Warns of Consequences," *New York Times*, September 17, 2020, http://nytimes.com/2020/09/17/world/asia/us-official -taiwan-china.html; Reuters, "U.S. Navy Rear Admiral Makes Unannounced Visit to Taiwan: Sources," November 22, 2020, http://reuters.com/article/us-taiwan-usa -military/u-s-navy-rear-admiral-makes-unannounced-visit-to-taiwan-sources -idUSKBN2820QW; and Julian E. Barnes and Amy Qin, "State Dept. Moves to Ease Restrictions on Meeting With Taiwan Officials," *New York Times*, January 9, 2021, http:// nytimes.com/2021/01/09/us/politics/state-dept-taiwan-united-states-china.html.

58. National Defense Authorization Act for Fiscal Year 2017, Pub. L. No. 114–328, 130 Stat. 2000, (2016); Taiwan Travel Act, Pub L. No. 115–135, 132 Stat. 341 (2018); and Consolidated Appropriations Act, 2021, 134 Stat. 279 (2020).

59. Thiessen, "Donald Trump Is the Most Pro-Taiwan President."

60. Reporters Without Borders, "2020 World Press Freedom Index," accessed December 17, 2020, http://rsf.org/en/ranking; and Walter Kerr and Macon Phillips, "Taiwan Is Beating Political Disinformation. The West Can Too," *Foreign Policy*, November 11, 2020, http://foreignpolicy.com/2020/11/11/political-disinformation-taiwan-success.

61. Lev Nachman, "Taiwan's Voters Show How to Beat Populism," *Foreign Policy*, January 13, 2020, http://foreignpolicy.com/2020/01/13/china-tsai-han-trump-boris-taiwans -voters-show-how-to-beat-populism.

62. Taiwan Foundation for Democracy, "2020 TFD Survey on Taiwanese View of Democratic Values and Governance," October 16, 2020, http://tfd.org.tw/opencms /english/events/data/Event0835.html.

63. Sidney Leng, "Taiwan's 2020 Economic Growth Looks to Outpace Mainland China's for First Time in Decades," *South China Morning Post*, December 12, 2020, http:// scmp.com/economy/china-economy/article/3113603/taiwans-2020-economic-growth -looks-outpace-mainland-chinas; and Economist Intelligence Unit, "Things to Watch in Taiwan in 2021," in *Country Report Taiwan Edition*, December 2, 2020.

64. "Taiwan Records Historical High in Exports in 2020," Focus Taiwan, January 8, 2021, http://focustaiwan.tw/business/202101080019.

65. Economist Intelligence Unit, "Things to Watch in Taiwan in 2021."

66. See Ruchir Sharma, "Pound for Pound, Taiwan Is the Most Important Place in the World," *New York Times*, December 14, 2020, http://nytimes.com/2020/12/14/opinion /taiwan-computer-chips.html.

67. David Pierson and Michelle Yun, "The Most Important Company You've Never Heard of Is Being Dragged Into the U.S.-China Rivalry," *Los Angeles Times*, December 17, 020, http://latimes.com/world-nation/story/2020-12-17/taiwan-chips-tsmc-china -us; Pan Tzu-yu and Elizabeth Hsu, "Taiwan's GDP Forecast to Hit 2.71% in 2020, 4.24% in 2021," Focus Taiwan, December 16, 2020, http://focustaiwan.tw/business /202012160022; and Economist Intelligence Unit, "Briefing Sheet," in *Country Report Taiwan Edition*, December 2, 2020.

68. For a comprehensive analysis of Taiwan's economic situation, see Evan A. Feigenbaum, *Assuring Taiwan's Innovation Future* (Washington, DC: Carnegie Endowment for International Peace, 2020), 9–11, http://carnegieendowment.org/2020/01/29/ assuring-taiwan-s-innovation-future-pub-80920.

69. *Statistical Yearbook of the Republic of China: 2019*, Directorate-General of Budget, Accounting and Statistics, September 2020, 30, http://eng.stat.gov.tw/public/data /dgbas03/bs2/yearbook_eng/Yearbook2019.pdf.

70. "Taiwan Population Fell for First Time in 2020," Agence France-Presse, January 8, 2021, http://france24.com/en/live-news/20210108-taiwan-population-fell-for-first -time-in-2020.

71. Lee Shen-yi, "The Nation Must Stop the Decline in Birthrate," *Taipei Times*, October 11, 2020, http://taipeitimes.com/News/editorials/archives/2020/10/11/2003744963.

72. See Feigenbaum, *Assuring Taiwan's Innovation Future*, 16, 11–14, 21–22, 24.

73. Richard Bernstein, "Assassinating Chiang Kai-shek," *Foreign Policy*, September 3, 2015, http://foreignpolicy.com/2015/09/03/assassinating-chiang-kai-shek-china -taiwan-japan-world-war-2.

74. President Chiang Kai-shek materials, 005-010205-00075-005, Academia Historica, Taipei, translation quoted in Haruka Matsumoto, "Chiang Kai-shek's Vision for Returning to China in the 1950s," Institute of Developing Economies Discussion Paper, Chiba, Japan, November 2018, http://ir.ide.go.jp/?action=repository_uri&item _id=50653&file_id=22&file_no=1.

75. Yang Hengjun, "Chiang Ching-kuo, China's Democratic Pioneer," *Diplomat*, December 10, 2014, http://thediplomat.com/2014/12/chiang-ching-kuo-chinas -democratic-pioneer.

76. Lee Teng-hui, "Interview of Taiwan President Lee Teng-hui With Deutsche Welle Radio," Deutsche Welle Radio, July 9, 1999, http://taiwandc.org/nws-9926.htm.

77. Chen Shui-bian, "Taiwan Stands Up: Presidential Inauguration Address" (speech, Taipei, May 20, 2000), http://china.usc.edu/chen-shui-bian-%E2%80%9Ctaiwan -stands-presidential-inauguration-address%E2%80%9D-may-20-2000.

78. CNN, "Chen Stands Up to Bush," Wednesday, December 10, 2003, http://edition.cnn .com/2003/WORLD/asiapcf/east/12/10/taiwan.us.china/index.html; Keith Bradsher, "Taiwan's Leader Tones Down Referendum Opposed by Beijing," *New York Times*, January 17, 2004, http://nytimes.com/2004/01/17/world/taiwan-s-leader-tones-down -referendum-opposed-by-beijing.html; and Unrepresented Nations and Peoples Organization, "Taiwan: Results of Referendum and Presidential Elections," March 22, 2004, http://unpo.org/article/470.

79. Ma Ying-jeou, "Inaugural Address" (speech, Taipei, May 20, 2008), http://china.usc .edu/ma-ying-jeou-%E2%80%9Cinaugural-address%E2%80%9D-may-20-2008.

80. Ming-sho Ho, "The Activist Legacy of Taiwan, Sunflower Movement," Carnegie Endowment for International Peace, August 2, 2018, http://carnegieendowment. org/2018/08/02/activist-legacy-of-taiwan-s-sunflower-movement-pub-76966.

81. See Richard C. Bush, "Tsai's Inauguration in Taiwan: It Could Have Been Worse," Brookings Institution, May 23, 2016, http://brookings.edu/blog/order-from-chaos /2016/05/23/tsais-inauguration-in-taiwan-it-could-have-been-worse.

82. Taiwan Mainland Affairs Council, "Percentage Distribution of the Questionnaire for the Survey on 'Public Views on Current Cross-Strait Issues,'" November 12, 2020, 4–5, http://ws.mac.gov.tw/001/Upload/297/relfile/8010/6039/7e7ec997-7d6c-48df -bb51-90994891b671.pdf.

83. Kat Devlin and Christine Huang, *In Taiwan, Views of Mainland China Mostly Negative*, Pew Research Center, May 12, 2020, 6, http://pewresearch.org/global/wp-content /uploads/sites/2/2020/05/PG_2020.05.12_Taiwan_final.pdf.

84. Dennis V. Hickey, "More and More Taiwanese Favor Independence – and Think the US Would Help Fight for It," *Diplomat*, December 3, 2020, http://thediplomat.com /2020/12/more-and-more-taiwanese-favor-independence-and-think-the-us-would -help-fight-for-it.

85. Taiwan Mainland Affairs Council, "Percentage Distribution of the Questionnaire for the Survey on 'Public Views on Current Cross-Strait Issues,'" November 12, 2020, 6,

http://ws.mac.gov.tw/001/Upload/297/relfile/8010/6039/7e7ec997-7d6c-48df-bb51
-90994891b671.pdf.

86. Devlin and Huang, *In Taiwan, Views of Mainland*, 3–4.

87. Cited in Hickey, "More and More Taiwanese Favor Independence."

88. We are especially grateful for the helpful suggestions on this section by Dr. Patricia M. Kim.

89. Mao apparently became less urgently concerned about Taiwan toward the end of his life. In 1975 he told Kissinger, "if you were to send it [Taiwan] back to me now, I would not want it, because it's not wantable. There are a huge bunch of counter-revolutionaries there. A hundred years hence we will want it (gesturing with his hand), and we are going to fight for it." "Memorandum of Conversation between Mao Zedong and Henry A. Kissinger," Gerald R. Ford Presidential Library, October 21, 1975, 4, http://digitalarchive .wilsoncenter.org/document/118072.

90. U.S. Department of State, *Foreign Relations of the United States*, Document 139, 368, http://history.state.gov/historicaldocuments/frus1969-76v17/d139.

91. Following the 1979–80 abrogation of the U.S.-ROC mutual defense treaty, Beijing for a few years changed its approach of "liberating Taiwan" to "peaceful reunification" under the One Country, Two Systems framework.

92. *China Daily*, "Deng Xiaoping on 'One Country, Two Systems,'" June 23, 1984, http:// chinadaily.com.cn/english/doc/2004-02/19/content_307590.htm.

93. Edward Friedman, "China's Changing Taiwan Policy," *American Journal of Chinese Studies* 14, no. 2 (October 2007): 125, http://jstor.org/stable/pdf/44288853.pdf. In this period, Jiang Zemin made an eight-point proposal that opposed deviations from the One China principle; noted Taiwan's efforts to establish nongovernmental ties with countries and to join international organizations while opposing expanded links that would challenge one China; proposed negotiations on "peaceful reunification"; clarified that Beijing's retention of the option to use force was directed not at "compatriots in Taiwan but against the schemes of foreign forces to interfere with China's reunification and to bring about the 'independence of Taiwan'"; encouraged efforts to establish cross-strait commercial, postal, air, and shipping links; implored Taiwanese and Chinese citizens to carry on their shared cultural inheritance; said that the "legitimate rights and interests" of Taiwanese should be respected; and stated that "leaders of the Taiwan authorities are welcome to pay visits in appropriate capacities." Jiang Zemin, "Continue to Promote the Reunification of the Motherland" (speech, Beijing, January 30, 1995), http://fmprc.gov.cn/mfa_eng/ljzg_665465/3568_665529 /t17784.shtml.

94. Patrick E. Tyler, "China Warns U.S. to Keep Away From Taiwan Strait," *New York Times*, March 18, 1996, http://nytimes.com/1996/03/18/world/china-warns-us-to -keep-away-from-taiwan-strait.html.

95. Anti-Secession Law of the People's Republic of China, (2005), Embassy of the People's Republic of China, http://china-embassy.org/eng/zt/999999999/t187406.htm.

96. Jing Huang, "Xi Jinping's Taiwan Policy: Boxing Taiwan In with the One-China Framework," in *Taiwan and China: Fitful Embrace*, edited by Dittmer Lowell (Oakland:

University of California Press, 2017), 239–48, http://jstor.org/stable/10.1525/j
.ctt1w76wpm.16.

97. Reuters, "China's Xi Says Political Solution for Taiwan Can't Wait Forever," October
6, 2013, http://reuters.com/article/us-asia-apec-china-taiwan/chinas-xi-says-political
-solution-for-taiwan-cant-wait-forever-idUSBRE99503Q20131006.

98. Javier C. Hernandez, "China Suspends Diplomatic Contact With Taiwan," *New York
Times*, June 25, 2016, http://nytimes.com/2016/06/26/world/asia/china-suspends
-diplomatic-contact-with-taiwan.html.

99. For a list of Beijing's actions see Richard C. Bush, "Danger Ahead? Taiwan's Politics,
China's Ambitions, and US Policy" (speech, Bloomington, Indiana, April 15, 2019),
http://brookings.edu/on-the-record/danger-ahead-taiwans-politics-chinas-ambitions
-and-us-policy.

100. Bush, "Tsai's Inauguration in Taiwan."

101. This list draws on Richard Bush's succinct summary of Beijing's conception of One
China, Two Systems. See "From Persuasion to Coercion: Beijing's Approach to Taiwan
and Taiwan's Response," Brookings Institution, November 2019, 2, http://brookings
.edu/wp-content/uploads/2019/11/FP_20191120_beijing_taiwan_bush.pdf.

102. Charlotte Gao, "Was It Wise for Tsai Ing-wen to Reject the '1992 Consensus'
Publicly?," *Diplomat*, January 4, 2019, http://thediplomat.com/2019/01/was-it-wise
-for-tsai-ing-wen-to-reject-the-1992-consensus-publicly.

103. Anna Fifield, "Taiwan's President Wins Second Term With Landslide Victory Over
Pro-Beijing Rival," *Washington Post*, January 15, 2020, http://washingtonpost.com
/world/asia_pacific/taiwanese-motivated-by-the-lessons-of-hong-kong-turn-out-in
-droves-to-vote/2020/01/11/6543228a-3138-11ea-971b-43bec3ff9860_story.html.

104. Devlin and Huang, *In Taiwan, Views of Mainland China*, 12. Additionally, two 2020
surveys show that more than 60 percent of Taiwanese respondents doubt the prospects
of unification with China in the next ten years, an increasing amount report worsening
views of the PRC, and a plurality say that independence is more likely than unification.
Huang Tzu-ti, "66% of Taiwanese See No Unification With China in Next Decade,"
Taiwan News, November 30, 2020, http://taiwannews.com.tw/en/news/4065824; and
Hickey, "More and More Taiwanese Favor Independence." See also Dennis Yuen Li,
"Cross Strait Relations in Pandemic Times," *Asia Report*, no. 49 (November 2020):
2–4, http://risingpowersinitiative.org/wp-content/uploads/AR-49-Cross-Strait
-Relations-in-Pandemic-Times.pdf.

105. See also Michael Green and Evan Medeiros, "Is Taiwan the Next Hong Kong?: China
Tests the Limits of Impunity," *Foreign Affairs*, July 8, 2020, http://foreignaffairs.com
/articles/east-asia/2020-07-08/taiwan-next-hong-kong.

106. John Lee, "Why Does China Fear Taiwan?," *American Interest*, November 6, 2015,
http://the-american-interest.com/2015/11/06/why-does-china-fear-taiwan.

107. Taiwan Travel Act, Pub L. No. 115–135, 132 Stat. 341 (2018); Taiwan Allies
International Protection and Enhancement Initiative (TAIPEI) Act of 2019, Pub. L.
No. 116–135 (2020); Consolidated Appropriations Act, 2021, 134 Stat. 279, (2020).

108. Formosan Association for Public Affairs, "Senate Taiwan Caucus," accessed January 13, 2021 http://fapa.org/senate-taiwan-caucus; and Formosan Association for Public Affairs, "House Taiwan Caucus," accessed January 13, 2021, http://fapa.org/house-taiwan-caucus.

109. Michael J. Green, Jude Blanchette, Bonnie Glaser, Hannah Fodale, Matthew Funaiole, Scott Kennedy, Louis Lauter, and Nicholas Szechenyi, "Mapping The Future of U.S. China Policy," Center for Strategic and International Studies, http://chinasurvey.csis.org.

110. For a Chinese article on the question, see "Peaceful Reunification With Taiwan Unlikely Without Pressure: Experts," *Global Times*, December 5, 2020, http://globaltimes.cn/content/1209043.shtml.

111. Xi Jinping, "Working Together to Realize Rejuvenation of the Chinese Nation and Advance China's Peaceful Reunification" (speech, Beijing, January 2, 2019), http://cfr.org/sites/default/files/pdf/1-2-19_working-together-to-realize-rejuvenation.pdf.

112. Steven Lee Myers, "China Sends Warning to Taiwan and U.S. With Big Show of Air Power," *New York Times*, September 18, 2020, http://nytimes.com/2020/09/18/world/asia/us-taiwan-china-jets.html.

113. Gerry Shih, "China Threatens Invasion of Taiwan In New Video Showing Military Might," *Washington Post*, October 12, 2020, http://washingtonpost.com/world/asia_pacific/china-taiwan-invasion-military-exercise/2020/10/12/291f5d86-0c58-11eb-b404-8d1e675ec701_story.html.

114. Ryan Hass, "Ryan Hass on Taiwan: Tsai's Steadiness Should Set the Tone," *Taipei Times*, August 10, 2020, http://taipeitimes.com/News/editorials/archives/2020/08/10/2003741401.

115. Jessie Yeung, "China Is Doubling Down on Its Territorial Claims and That's Causing Conflict Across Asia," CNN, September 30, 2020, http://cnn.com/2020/09/26/asia/china-asia-territorial-claims-conflicts-explainer-intl-hnk-scli/index.html; and Green and Medeiros, "Is Taiwan the Next Hong Kong?"

116. Bush, "From Persuasion to Coercion"; and Bonnie Glaser and Matthew P. Funaiole, "China's Provocations Around Taiwan Aren't a Crisis," *Foreign Policy*, May 15, 2020, http://foreignpolicy.com/2020/05/15/chinas-provocations-around-taiwan-arent-a-crisis. See also John Feng, "Bullish China Vows Continued Push for Taiwan 'Unification' in 2021," *Newsweek*, December 30, 2021, http://newsweek.com/bullish-china-vows-continued-push-taiwan-unification-2021-1557994.

117. See Bush, "From Persuasion to Coercion," 5–6.

118. For a recent summary of Chinese activity swirling around Taiwan, see Ying-Yu Lin, "China's Military Actions Against Taiwan in 2021: What to Expect," *Diplomat*, December 18, 2020, http://thediplomat.com/2020/12/chinas-military-actions-against-taiwan-in-2021-what-to-expect. For a good introduction to Chinese views of their naval and maritime situation, see Toshi Yoshihara and James R. Holmes, *Red Star Over the Pacific: China's Rise and the Challenge to U.S. Maritime Strategy*, 2nd ed. (Annapolis: Naval Institute Press, 2018); complemented by Andrew S. Erickson and Joel Wuthnow, "Barriers, Springboards and Benchmarks: China Conceptualizes the Pacific 'Island Chains,'" *China Quarterly* 225 (March 2016): 1–22.

119. Yimou Lee, David Lague, and Ben Blanchard, "China Launches 'Gray-Zone' Warfare to Subdue Taiwan," Reuters, December 10, 2020, http://reuters.com/investigates/special-report/hongkong-taiwan-military.

120. See Lo Tien-pin and William Hetherington, "PLA Drill Spurs Deployment of Troops to Pratas," *Taipei Times*, August 5, 2020, http://taipeitimes.com/News/front/archives/2020/08/05/2003741143; and Lawrence Chung, "Taiwan Sends Marines to Reinforce South China Sea Outpost Amid Reports of Major PLA Landing Drill," *South China Morning Post*, August 5, 2020, http://scmp.com/news/china/military/article/3096004/taiwan-sends-marines-reinforce-south-china-sea-outpost-amid.

121. Yew Lun Tian, "China Authorizes Coast Guard to Fire on Foreign Vessels as Needed," Reuters, January 22, 2021, http://reuters.com/article/us-china-coastguard-law/china-authorises-coast-guard-to-fire-on-foreign-vessels-if-needed-idUSKBN29R1ER.

122. See, for example, "China's Maritime Expansion Reflects a Curious Mix of Ambition and Paranoia," *Economist*, July 6, 2019, http://economist.com/china/2019/07/06/chinas-maritime-expansion-reflects-a-curious-mix-of-ambition-and-paranoia; see also Yoshihara and Holmes, *Red Star*, 48–140.

123. For a useful overview of the historical challenge of amphibious assault, see Paul Kennedy, *Engineers of Victory* (New York: Random House, 2013), 215–82. For a fine current overview of the Taiwan defense problem, see Michael A. Hunzeker and Alexander Lanoszka, *A Question of Time: Enhancing Taiwan's Conventional Deterrence Posture*, Center for Security Policy Studies at George Mason University, November 2018, http://csps.gmu.edu/wp-content/uploads/2018/11/A-Question-of-Time.pdf. See generally, for relatively upbeat appraisals of Taiwan's intrinsic advantages, in theory, Ian Easton, *The Chinese Invasion Threat: Taiwan's Defense and American Strategy in Asia* (Manchester, UK: Eastbridge, 2019); Tanner Greer, "Taiwan Can Win a War With China," *Foreign Policy*, September 25, 2018, http://foreignpolicy.com/2018/09/25/taiwan-can-win-a-war-with-china. Even more optimistic, see Mike Sweeney, "Assessing Chinese Maritime Power," Defense Priorities, October 2020, http://static1.squarespace.com/static/56a146abb204d5878d6f125a/t/5fc86d006652ad59ec28b952/1606970627597/DEFP_Assessing_Chinese_maritime_power.pdf.

124. For a major recent analysis of these intrinsic theoretical advantages in evolving military technology, see Michael Beckley, "The Emerging Military Balance in East Asia: How China's Neighbors Can Check Chinese Naval Expansion," *International Security* 42, no. 2 (2017): 78–119. Beckley's article prompted correspondence and replies in which Beckley sustained his argument. See also Toshihara and Holmes, *Red Star*, 220–47. T. X. Hammes referred to this technological trend as "The Future of Warfare: Small, Many, Smart vs. Few & Exquisite," *War on the Rocks*, July 16, 2014, http://warontherocks.com/2014/07/the-future-of-warfare-small-many-smart-vs-few-exquisite.

On Flournoy's statement, see Michèle A. Flournoy, "How to Prevent a War in Asia," *Foreign Affairs*, June 18, 2020, http://foreignaffairs.com/articles/united-states/2020-06-18/how-prevent-war-asia; for Work's articulation of the idea, see Sydney Freedberg Jr., "US 'Gets Its Ass Handed to It' In Wargames: Here's a $24 Billion Fix," Breaking Defense, March 7, 2019, http://breakingdefense.com/2019/03/us-gets-its-ass-handed-to-it-in-wargames-heres-a-24-billion-fix.

125. See Mark Cancian, "The Marine Corps' Radical Shift toward China," Center for Strategic and International Studies, March 25, 2020, http://csis.org/analysis/marine-corps-radical-shift-toward-china.

126. Good recent analyses of this kind include Thomas G. Mahnken, Travis Sharp, Billy Fabian, and Peter Kouretsos, *Tightening the Chain: Implementing a Strategy of Maritime Pressure in the Western Pacific* (Washington, DC: Center for Strategic and Budgetary Assessments, 2019), http://csbaonline.org/research/publications/implementing-a-strategy-of-maritime-pressure-in-the-western-pacific/publication/1; Beckley, "China Keeps Inching Closer to Taiwan"; "Defending Taiwan Is Growing Costlier and Deadlier," *Economist*,; October 10, 2020, http://economist.com/asia/2020/10/10/defending-taiwan-is-growing-costlier-and-deadlier, James Holmes, "Taiwan Needs a Maoist Military," *Foreign Policy*, October 17, 2019, http://foreignpolicy.com/2019/10/17/taiwan-maoist-military-china-navy-south-china-sea; and Colin Carroll and Rebecca Friedman Lissner, "Forget the Subs: What Taipei Can Learn From Tehran About Asymmetric Defense," *War on the Rocks*, April 6, 2017, http://warontherocks.com/2017/04/forget-the-subs-what-taipei-can-learn-from-tehran-about-asymmetric-defense.

127. Hunzeker and Lanoszka, *A Question of Time*, has a good analysis of the limitations; see also, for example, Michael Beckley, "China Keeps Inching Closer to Taiwan," *Foreign Policy*, October 19, 2020, http://foreignpolicy.com/2020/10/19/china-keeps-inching-closer-to-taiwan; and Paul Huang, "Taiwan's Military Is a Hollow Shell," *Foreign Policy*, February 15, 2020, http://foreignpolicy.com/2020/02/15/china-threat-invasion-conscription-taiwans-military-is-a-hollow-shell. For an older critique that summarized the long-term decline in Taiwan's defenses, see Michael Mazza, "Taiwanese Hard Power: Between a ROC and a Hard Place," American Enterprise Institute, April 2014, http://aei.org/wp-content/uploads/2014/04/-taiwanese-hard-power-between-a-roc-and-a-hard-place_092826925958.pdf.

128. See also "President Tsai Ing-Wen's Statements and Guidance of National Defense," in ROC Ministry of National Defense, *National Defense Report 2019* (Taipei: MND, 2019), 64.

129. Lee Hsi-ming quoted in Lee, Lague, and Blanchard, "China Launches."

130. A classic essay is Marc Trachtenberg's "A 'Wasting Asset': American Strategy and the Shifting Nuclear Balance, 1949–1954," in *History and Strategy* (Princeton, NJ: Princeton University Press, 1991), 100–52.

131. Van Jackson, "Grappling with the Fait Accompli: A Classical Tactic in the Modern Strategic Landscape," *War on the Rocks*, May 31, 2016, http://warontherocks.com/2016/05/grappling-with-the-fait-accompli-a-classical-tactic-in-the-modern-strategic-landscape.

132. Holmes, "Taiwan Needs a Maoist Military."

133. NSC (Pottinger/McMaster), "U.S. Strategic Framework for the Indo-Pacific," 7, 5, http://news.usni.org/2021/01/15/u-s-strategic-framework-for-the-indo-pacific.

134. Lyle Goldstein, "Storm Clouds Are Gathering Over the Taiwan Strait," *National Interest*, July 18, 2018, http://nationalinterest.org/feature/storm-clouds-are-gathering-over-taiwan-strait-26146. In this article and elsewhere, Goldstein refers to this scenario as a "Cuban Missile Crisis in reverse." He means this in the sense of sizing up the local military balance, not as an analysis of the quarantine scenario we discussed earlier.

135. For a good brief overview of the American commitment to Berlin, see Ernest May, "America's Berlin: Heart of the Cold War," *Foreign Affairs* 77, no. 4 (1998): 148–60. For a recent analysis of how Soviet deployments of missiles to Cuba in 1962 were related to the climactic phase of the crisis over Berlin, trying to deflate the American threat to escalate a conflict over Berlin, see Philip Zelikow, "'Documentary Evidence' and Llewellyn Thompson's Analysis of Soviet Motives in the October 1962 Missile Crisis," *H-Diplo Commentary*, December 2018, http://issforum.org/essays/PDF/CR2.pdf.

136. See Gideon Rachman, "A New Cold War: Trump, Xi and the Escalating US-China Confrontation," *Financial Times*, October 5, 2020, http://ft.com/content/7b809c6a -f733-46f5-a312-9152aed28172; Alan Dupont, "The US-China Cold War Has Already Started," *Diplomat*, July 8, 2020, http://thediplomat.com/2020/07/the-us -china-cold-war-has-already-started; and Charles Edel and Hal Brands, "The Real Origins of the U.S.-China Cold War," *Foreign Policy*, June 2, 2019, http://foreignpolicy .com/2019/06/02/the-real-origins-of-the-u-s-china-cold-war-big-think-communism.

137. See Philip Zelikow, "The Nature of History's Lessons," in *The Power of the Past: History and Statecraft*, edited by Hal Brands and Jeremi Suri (Washington, DC: Brookings Institution, 2016), 281–310.

138. Among the excellent histories of the Czechoslovakia crisis of 1938, the aspects mentioned in this report are drawn out in recent works by Zara Steiner, *The Triumph of the Dark: European International History, 1933–1939* (Oxford: Oxford University Press, 2013); Ernest May, *Strange Victory: Hitler's Conquest of France* (New York: Farrar, Strauss & Giroux, 2000) (which has much about this crisis); Donald Cameron Watt, *How War Came: The Immediate Origins of the Second World War, 1938–1939* (New York: Pantheon, 1989); P. E. Caquet, *The Bell of Treason: The 1938 Munich Agreement in Czechoslovakia* (London: Other Press, 2019); and Tim Bouverie, *Appeasement: Chamberlain, Hitler, Churchill, and the Road to War* (New York: Tim Duggan Books, 2019).

139. For a selection of the many factors a Biden administration should consider regarding U.S. relations with China and Taiwan, see Patrick Mendis and Corey Lee Bell, "Leave Donald Trump's Triumphant Taiwan Policy Alone," *National Interest*, December 12, 2020, http://nationalinterest.org/feature/leave-donald-trump%E2%80%99s -triumphant-taiwan-policy-alone-174298; Lucy Best and Yanzhong Huang, "COVID-19 Yields a Sharper Picture of China-Taiwan Relations," *Georgetown Journal of International Affairs*, December 7, 2020, http://gjia.georgetown.edu/2020/12/07/covid-19 -yields-a-sharper-picture-of-china-taiwan-relations; and Javier C. Hernandez and Amy Chang Chien, "After Trump, Biden Faces Pressure to Stand Up to China by Embracing Taiwan," *New York Times*, November 24, 2020, http://nytimes.com/2020/11/24/world /asia/taiwan-china-trump-biden.html. See also "Ryan Hass on Taiwan: A Case for Optimism on US-Taiwan Relations," *Taipei Times*, November 30, 2020, http://taipei-times.com/News/editorials/archives/2020/11/30/2003747816.

140. John Locke, "Of Power," in *The Works of John Locke in Nine Volumes*, 12th ed. (London: Rivington, 1824), 1, 264, http://oll.libertyfund.org/titles/761#Locke_0128-01_918.

141. U.S. Department of State, *Foreign Relations of the United States*, Document 203, http:// history.state.gov/historicaldocuments/frus1969-76v17/d203.

142. Michael R. Pompeo, interview by Hugh Hewitt, *Hugh Hewitt Show*, November 12, 2020, http://state.gov/secretary-michael-r-pompeo-with-hugh-hewitt-of-the-hugh

-hewitt-show-7. Leaders in Beijing were predictably incensed. Reuters, "China Warns of Action After Pompeo Says Taiwan Not Part of China," November 13, 2020, http:// uk.reuters.com/article/us-china-usa-taiwan-idUSKBN27T0XM.

143. Knowlton, "Bush Warns Taiwan to Keep Status Quo."

144. See Chas W. Freeman Jr., "War With China Over Taiwan?" (remarks to a Salon of the Committee of the Republic, Washington, DC, December 17, 2020), http:// chasfreeman.net/war-with-china-over-taiwan. For an earlier formulation of this concept, see Logan Wright, "Dual Deterrence: A New Taiwan Strategy," *National Interest*, March 31, 2004, http://nationalinterest.org/article/dual-deterrence-a-new -taiwan-strategy-2611.

145. Taiwan Relations Act of 1979, Pub. L. No. 98-6, 22 Stat. 14 (3301).

146. George Shultz to James Lilley, "Assurances for Taiwan," August 17, 1982, http://ait.org .tw/our-relationship/policy-history/key-u-s-foreign-policy-documents-region/six -assurances-1982.

147. Kelly Wallace, "Bush Pledges Whatever It Takes to Defend Taiwan," CNN, April 25, 2001, http://edition.cnn.com/2001/ALLPOLITICS/04/24/bush.taiwan.abc.

148. Donald J. Trump interviewed by Steve Hilton, *The Next Revolution*, 8:38–9:27, August 23, 2020, http://foxnews.com/media/trump-biden-china-decouple-trade-deal.

149. Richard Haass and David Sacks, "American Support for Taiwan Must Be Unambiguous: To Keep the Peace, Make Clear to China That Force Won't Stand," *Foreign Affairs*, September 2, 2020, http://foreignaffairs.com/articles/united-states/american-support -taiwan-must-be-unambiguous. Contrary to much of the subsequent commentary, a close reading of the Haass text demonstrates that he does not advocate a U.S. pledge to use military force in response to a Chinese attack on Taiwan. Rather, he wants to make clear that Washington would react, but in unspecified ways, and urges that it should redouble its efforts to be ready for the gamut of Taiwan contingencies, which is sensible advice in any case. See Bonnie S. Glaser, Michael J. Mazarr, Michael J. Glennon, Richard Haass, and David Sacks, "Dire Straits: Should American Support for Taiwan Be Ambiguous?" *Foreign Affairs*, September 24, 2020, http://foreignaffairs.com/articles /united-states/2020-09-24/dire-straits.

150. Michael R. Pompeo, "Communist China and the Free World's Future" (speech, Yorba Linda, CA, July 23, 2020), http://2017-2021.state.gov/communist-china-and-the -free-worlds-future-2/index.html. For a similar viewpoint about the incompatibility of the American and Chinese political systems, see Hal Brands, *Regime Realism and Chinese Grand Strategy* (Washington, DC: American Enterprise Institute, 2020), http://aei.org/wp-content/uploads/2020/11/Regime-Realism-and-Chinese-Grand -Strategy.pdf.

151. Philip H. Gordon, *Losing the Long Game: The False Promise of Regime Change in the Middle East* (New York: St. Martin's Press, 2020).

152. See Christian Whiton, "Time for Donald Trump to Visit Taiwan," *National Interest*, November 21, 2020, http://nationalinterest.org/feature/time-donald-trump-visit -taiwan-173110; John Bolton, "'The China Nightmare' Review: Beijing Never Got the Memo," *Wall Street Journal*, November 15, 2020, http://wsj.com/articles/the-china -nightmare-review-beijing-never-got-the-memo-11605476188; and Therese Shaheen,

"The Need to Clarify and Strengthen Our Relationship With Taiwan," *National Review*, September 11, 2019, http://nationalreview.com/2019/09/to-pressure-china-we-must-clarify-and-strengthen-our-relationship-with-taiwan. For a rebuttal to Bolton's call to leverage Taiwan against China, see Yoni Katz, "John Bolton and Avoiding a China-Taiwan War," letter, *Wall Street Journal*, November 22, 2020, http://wsj.com/articles/john-bolton-and-avoiding-a-china-taiwan-war-11606076329.

153. For an authoritative report on the subject, see Richard L. Armitage and Joseph S. Nye, *The U.S.-Japan Alliance in 2020: An Equal Alliance With a Global Agenda* (Washington, DC: Center for Strategic and International Studies, 2020), http://csis-website-prod.s3 .amazonaws.com/s3fs-public/publication/201204_Armitage_Nye_US_Japan_Alliance _1.pdf; Emerson Lim, "Taiwan, U.S., Japan Announce Priority Areas of Cooperation for 2021," Focus Taiwan, December 15, 2020, http://focustaiwan.tw/politics /202012150023; Ash Carter, "Reflections on American Grand Strategy in Asia," Belfer Center for Science and International Affairs, October 2018, http://belfercenter .org/publication/reflections-american-grand-strategy-asia; Douglas Feith and Gary Roughead, "China's Maritime Strategic Challenge," *National Review*, October 18, 2019, http://nationalreview.com/2019/10/china-maritime-threat-us-allies-must-work -together-to-meet-challenge; Andrew A. Michta, "As China Surges, Europe Is on the Menu," *American Interest*, September 11, 2019, http://the-american-interest.com /2019/09/11/as-china-surges-europe-is-on-the-menu; and Josh Rogin, "Trump and Europe Must Make Up and Work Together to Confront China," *Washington Post*, August 25, 2019, http://washingtonpost.com/opinions/2019/08/25/trump-europe -must-make-up-work-together-confront-china.

154. See Michael Mazza, "Strengthening Cooperation and Dialogue Between the United States, Europe, and Taiwan," American Enterprise Institute, May 8, 2020, http://aei .org/op-eds/strengthening-cooperation-and-dialogue-between-the-united-states -europe-and-taiwan.

155. See Ming-Yen Tsai, "Why Deepening EU-Taiwan Economic Ties Matter," *Diplomat*, November 12, 2020, http://thediplomat.com/2020/11/why-deepening-eu-taiwan -economic-ties-matter.

156. NHK, "Taiwan Denied Observer Status at WHO Assembly," November 9, 2020.

157. Chao Deng, "Taiwan Stopped Covid-19's Spread, but Can't Talk About It at WHO Meeting," *Wall Street Journal*, November 12, 2020, http://wsj.com/articles/taiwan -stopped-covid-19s-spread-but-cant-talk-about-it-at-who-meeting-11605182401.

158. Bonnie S. Glaser and Jacqueline A. Vitello, *Taiwan's Marginalized Role in International Security: Paying a Price* (Washington, DC: Center for Strategic and International Studies, 2015), 9–10, http://csis-website-prod.s3.amazonaws.com/s3fs-public/legacy _files/files/publication/150105_Glaser_TaiwanMarginalizedRole_WEB.pdf.

159. See Huang Ming-chao, "Taiwan Is Crucial to the Global Fight Against Cybercrime," *Manila Standard*, November 28, 2020, http://manilastandard.net/opinion/columns /everyman/340719/taiwan-is-crucial-to-the-global-fight-against-cybercrime.html.

160. See Grace Dean and Ben Blanchard, "Taiwanese Politicians Threw Punches and Pig Guts in Parliament in Bitter Dispute Over U.S. Pork Imports," *Business Insider*, November 27, 2020, http://businessinsider.com/taiwan-politicians-throw-punches -pig-guts-over-us-pork-imports-2020-11.

161. Chun Han Wong and William Kazer, "Taiwan's Opposition Party Reconsiders Support for Closer China Ties," *Wall Street Journal*, March 8, 2020, http://wsj.com/articles/taiwans -opposition-party-reviews-its-support-for-closer-china-ties-11583673325.

162. American Institute in Taiwan and Taiwan Economic and Cultural Representative Office in the United States, *AIT-TECRO Mutual Legal Assistance Agreement* (Washington, DC, 2002), http://ait.org.tw/wp-content/uploads/sites/269/2016/12/20020326-mutual -legal-assistance-agreement.pdf; and *Taipei Times*, "Taiwanese-US-Thai Operation Nets 95kg of Drugs in Bangkok," July 18, 2019, http://taipeitimes.com/News/taiwan/archives /2019/07/18/2003718896.

163. For a concurring view, see Kerr and Phillips, "Taiwan Is Beating Political Disinformation. The West Can Too."

164. Although Washington and Taipei's economic collaboration can bring benefits to the two sides, the U.S. decision to forbid chip-makers who use American technology from supplying chips to Huawei could force Taiwanese companies to choose between American and Chinese profits. See Sherisse Pham, "Taiwan Chip Maker TSMC's $12 Billion Arizona Factory Could Give the U.S. an Edge in Manufacturing," CNN, May 15, 2020, http://cnn.com/2020/05/15/tech/tsmc-arizona-chip-factory-intl-hnk/index .html; Jackie Northam, "A Taiwanese Company That Got Caught in the Middle of Tech War," NPR, May 26, 2020, http://npr.org/2020/05/26/862654151/a-taiwanese -company-that-got-caught-in-the-middle-of-tech-war; and "Why Commercial Ties Between Taiwan and China are Beginning to Fray," *Economist*, November 19, 2020, http://economist.com/business/2020/11/19/why-commercial-ties-between-taiwan -and-china-are-beginning-to-fray.

165. See Rob Spalding, "Heart to Heart: How the U.S. and Taiwan Can Save the Chip Industry From China," *RealClear Defense*, November 12, 2020, http://realcleardefense. com/articles/2020/11/12/heart_to_heart_how_the_us_and_taiwan_can_save_the _chip_industry_from_china_583796.html. For an account of TSMC's vital role in the international chip market, see John Lee and Jan-Peter Kleinhans, "Taiwan, Chips, and Geopolitics: Part 1," *Diplomat*, December 10, 2020, http://thediplomat.com/2020/12 /taiwan-chips-and-geopolitics-part-1.

166. See Feigenbaum, *Assuring Taiwan's Innovation Future*, 27–28; and William Brent Christensen, Jeffrey Tung, Arati Shroff, Chich-Ching Yang, and Stephen Su, "U.S.- Taiwan Forum on Pandemic Prevention and Supply Chain Restructuring" (panel discussion, Ministry of Economic Affairs and American Institute in Taiwan, Taipei, November 25, 2020), http://taiwannews.com.tw/en/news/4062726.

167. See Louise Watt, "With U.S. Cooperation, a Shift in Supply Chains," *Taiwan Business TOPICS*, October 15, 2020, http://topics.amcham.com.tw/2020/10/us-cooperation -supply-chain-shift.

168. See Feigenbaum, *Assuring Taiwan's Innovation Future*, 25–26.

169. Business Wire, "Taiwan Signs Agreement With Companies in USA, Japan, and South-east Asia to Champion AI for Business," November 12, 2020, http://businesswire.com /news/home/20201112005422/en; American Institute in Taiwan, "Fact Sheet To be Re-leased by AIT and TECRO on U.S.-Taiwan Economic Prosperity Partnership Dialogue," PR-2061, November 21, 2020, http://ait.org.tw/fact-sheet-by-ait-tecro-us-taiwan-eppd;

and Huizhong Wu, "US, Taiwan Step Up Economic Cooperation in New Dialogue," Associated Press, November 21, 2020, http://apnews.com/article/global-trade-financial-markets-china-taipei-bilateral-trade-20473f25562d37c58c4f554cefbb7df5.

170. International Trade Administration, "U.S. Goods Trade With Global Partners," accessed November 3, 2020, http://trade.gov/data-visualization/trading-partners-exports-and-imports; and David Brunnstrom, "U.S. to Hold Economic Talks With Taiwan This Month: Pompeo," Reuters, November 10, 2020, http://reuters.com/article/us-usa-taiwan-pompeo-idUSKBN27Q30D.

171. See Ashley J. Tellis, "Sign a Free-Trade Deal With Taiwan," *Wall Street Journal*, December 2, 2018, http://wsj.com/articles/sign-a-free-trade-deal-with-taiwan-1543786364; and Daniel Blumenthal and Michael Mazza, "A Golden Opportunity for a U.S.-Taiwan Free Trade Agreement," Project 2049 Institute, February 14, 2019, 11–12, http://aei.org/wp-content/uploads/2019/02/US_TW_Trade_Blumenthal_Mazza_P2049_021419.pdf.

172. See Blumenthal and Mazza, "A Golden Opportunity," 7–8.

173. For a similar view, see Kurt Tong, "Now Is the Right Time for a Trade Agreement with Taiwan," Center for Strategic and International Studies, May 27, 2020, http://csis.org/analysis/now-right-time-trade-agreement-taiwan.

174. Taiwan Allies International Protection and Enhancement Initiative (TAIPEI) Act of 2019, Pub. L. No. 116–135, 134 Stat. 278, http://congress.gov/bill/116th-congress/senate-bill/1678/all-info; Reuters, "50 U.S. Senators Call for Talks on Trade Agreement With Taiwan," October 1, 2020, http://reuters.com/article/us-usa-taiwan-china/50-u-s-senators-call-for-talks-on-trade-agreement-with-taiwan-idUSKBN26M7HL; and Tsai Ing-wen, "President Tsai Ing-wen Discusses the Diplomatic, Security, and Economic Challenges Facing Taiwan" (speech, Taipei, August 12, 2020), http://hudson.org/research/16300-transcript-president-tsai-ing-wen-discusses-the-diplomatic-security-and-economic-challenges-facing-taiwan. Support for a free trade agreement comes from a range of sources on both sides of the Pacific, but restrictions on U.S. pork and beef still arouse passionate opposition in Taiwan and friction in the House Ways and Means Committee and the office of the U.S. Trade Representative. A deal would also require coordination between Congress and the Executive Branch on how to sort out the legal details of a comprehensive trade agreement between two entities that do not have official relations. Task Force on U.S. Policy Toward Taiwan, *Toward a Stronger U.S.-Taiwan Relationship* (Washington, DC: Center for Strategic and International Studies, 2020), 11–13, http://csis-website-prod.s3.amazonaws.com/s3fs-public/publication/201021_Glaser_TaskForce_Toward_A_Stronger_USTaiwan_Relationship_0.pdf.

175. Reuters, "Taiwan Says on Track to Apply to Join Trans-Pacific Trade Pact," December 13, 2020, http://reuters.com/article/us-taiwan-trade/taiwan-says-on-track-to-apply-to-join-trans-pacific-trade-pact-idUSKBN28O015; and *Taiwan Today*, "President Tsai Reiterates Taiwan's Commitment to Joining CPTPP," September 4, 2019, http://taiwantoday.tw/news.php?unit=2,6,10,15,18&post=161571.

176. Michael Reilly, "Taiwan—TPP or not TPP?," Taiwan Insight, November 6, 2019, http://taiwaninsight.org/2019/11/06/taiwan-tpp-or-not-tpp.

177. For a similar view, see Pen Koon Heng, "Expanding the TPP?: Prospects for South Korea, Taiwan, and ASEAN," (event video, Woodrow Wilson Center, June 29, 2016),

1:01:00, http://wilsoncenter.org/event/expanding-the-tpp-prospects-for-south-korea
-taiwan-and-asean; and Reilly, "Taiwan – TPP or not TPP?"

178. Task Force on U.S. Policy Toward Taiwan, *Toward a Stronger U.S.-Taiwan Relationship*,
      9–10.

179. Ministry of Foreign Affairs Republic of China (Taiwan), "ROC Government
      Launches First Class at New Ebola Prevention Training Center," PR 046, March 18,
      2015, http://mofa.gov.tw/en/News_Content.aspx?n=539A9A50A5F8AF9E&s
      =55AAE3188F7230CC. For a similar view, see Kelley Lee and Jennifer Fang,
      "Challenges and Opportunities for Taiwan's Global Health Diplomacy," Brookings
      Institution, May 10, 2016, http://brookings.edu/opinions/challenges-and
      -opportunities-for-taiwans-global-health-diplomacy.

180. Lee I-chia, "Taiwan, US Sign Agreement on Health," *Taipei Times*, August 11, 2020,
      http://taipeitimes.com/News/taiwan/archives/2020/08/11/2003741481.

181. Joyce Huang, "Taiwan Plans to Help the US Shift Medical Supply Chain Away from
      China," Voice of America, August 13, 2020, http://voanews.com/east-asia-pacific
      /taiwan-plans-help-us-shift-medical-supply-chain-away-china.

182. See Ezekiel J. Emanuel, Cathy Zhang, and Aaron Glickman, "Learning From Taiwan
      About Responding To Covid-19 — and Using Electronic Health Records," STAT, June
      30, 2020, http://statnews.com/2020/06/30/taiwan-lessons-fighting-covid-19-using
      -electronic-health-records.

183. See Richard C. Bush, "The U.S.-Taiwan Relationship and People-to-People Ties"
      (panel discussion, Carnegie Endowment for International Peace, Washington, DC,
      June 27, 2017), 1:16:35–1:17:00, http://carnegieendowment.org/2017/06/27/u.s.
      -taiwan-relationship-and-people-to-people-ties-event-5624.

184. Although far fewer Americans study in Taiwan than in China, the 2018–19 academic
      year saw a 48 percent increase in the number of U.S. students in Taiwan. Institute
      of International Education, "All Places of Origin Data From the 2020 Open Doors
      Report," accessed December 3, 2020, http://opendoorsdata.org/data/international
      -students/all-places-of-origin; and "U.S. Study Abroad Data From the 2020 Open
      Doors Report," accessed December 3, 2020, http://opendoorsdata.org/data/us-study
      -abroad/all-destinations.

185. See Sebra Yen, "Securing the Future With More U.S.-Taiwan Exchange Programs,"
      Project 2049 Institute, December 7, 2016, http://project2049.net/2016/12/07
      /securing-the-future-with-more-u-s-taiwan-exchange-programs.

186. Brent Christensen and Joseph Wu, "U.S.-Taiwan Joint Statement," PR-2009, American
      Institute in Taiwan, March 18, 2020, http://ait.org.tw/u-s-taiwan-joint-statement.

187. For a similar view, see Jessica Batke, "Does China's Foreign NGO Law Present a Non-
      profit Opportunity for Taiwan?," China File, July 25, 2018, http://chinafile.com/ngo
      /analysis/does-chinas-foreign-ngo-law-present-non-profit-opportunity-taiwan.

188. Multiple 2020 Pew surveys revealed that 78 percent of Americans said China's
      initial virus response was a "great deal" or "fair amount" to blame for the pandemic's
      spread; a decreasing amount are in favor of a stronger trade relationship with China;
      77 percent have "not too much confidence" or "no confidence at all" in Xi Jinping

to "do the right thing" in world affairs; and 82 percent viewed PRC human rights policies as a very or somewhat serious problem for the United States. Laura Silver, Kat Devlin, and Christine Huang, "Americans Fault China for Its Role in the Spread of COVID-19," Pew Research Center, July 30, 2020, 3, 4, 14, 19, http://pewresearch.org/global/2020/07/30/americans-fault-china-for-its-role-in-the-spread-of-covid-19; and "U.S. Views of China Increasingly Negative Amid Coronavirus Outbreak," Pew Research Center, April 21, 2020, 10, http://pewresearch.org/global/2020/04/21/u-s-views-of-china-increasingly-negative-amid-coronavirus-outbreak.

189. See Gregory Kulacki, "Would China Use Nuclear Weapons First in a War With the United States?," *Diplomat*, April 27, 2020, http://thediplomat.com/2020/04/would-china-use-nuclear-weapons-first-in-a-war-with-the-united-states; Andreas Kluth, "The Risk of Nuclear Proliferation (and War) Is Growing," Bloomberg, January 9, 2020, http://bloomberg.com/opinion/articles/2020-01-09/game-theory-shows-risk-of-nuclear-war-is-growing-with-iran-rift; David C. Gompert, Astrid Stuth Cevallos, and Cristina L. Garafola, *War With China: Thinking Through the Unthinkable* (Santa Monica, CA: RAND Corporation, 2016), IX, http://rand.org/content/dam/rand/pubs/research_reports/RR1100/RR1140/RAND_RR1140.pdf; and Michael Mazza and Henry Sokolski, "China's Nuclear Arms Are a Riddle Wrapped in a Mystery," *Foreign Policy*, March 13, 2020, http://foreignpolicy.com/2020/03/13/china-nuclear-arms-race-mystery.

190. Gompert, Cevallos, and Garafola, *War With China*, 33; and Robert Farley, "Forget North Korea: A War Between China and America Would Be a World War," *National Interest*, December 29, 2017, http://nationalinterest.org/blog/the-buzz/forget-north-korea-war-between-china-america-would-be-world-23862.

191. See Grant Newsham, "Taiwan War: Global Economic, Psychological Damage," *Asia Times,* January 16, 2020, http://asiatimes.com/2020/01/taiwan-war-global-economic-psychological-damage.

192. For an assessment of the economic effects of a U.S-China war see Gompert, Cevallos, and Garafola, *War With China*, 41–50.

193. For an analysis of the effects and uncertainties of cyberwar directed at the United States, see Thomas M. Eisenbach, Anna Kovner, and Michael Junho Lee, *Cyber Risk and the U.S. Financial System: A Pre-Mortem Analysis* (New York: Federal Reserve Bank of New York, 2020), http://newyorkfed.org/medialibrary/media/research/staff_reports/sr909.pdf; Lloyd's Emerging Risk Report – 2015 (London: Lloyd's of London and Cambridge University Center for Risk Studies, 2015), 4, 16 http://jbs.cam.ac.uk/wp-content/uploads/2020/08/crs-lloyds-business-blackout-scenario.pdf; and Gompert, Cevallos, and Garafola, *War With China*, 48–50.

194. David E. Sanger, David Barboza, and Nicole Perlroth, "Chinese Army Unit Is Seen as Tied to Hacking Against U.S.," *New York Times*, February 18, 2013, http://nytimes.com/2013/02/19/technology/chinas-army-is-seen-as-tied-to-hacking-against-us.html.

195. Zak Doffman, "Chinese State Hackers Suspected Of Malicious Cyber Attack On U.S. Utilities," *Forbes*, August 3, 2019, http://forbes.com/sites/zakdoffman/2019/08/03/chinese-state-hackers-suspected-of-malicious-cyber-attack-on-u-s-utilities.

196.   Dustin Volz and Robert McMillan, "Hackers Hit Hospitals in Disruptive Ransomware Attack," *Wall Street Journal*, October 29, 2020, http://wsj.com/articles/hackers-hit-hospitals-in-disruptive-ransomware-attack-11603992735.

197.   For a recounting of U.S. cyber vulnerabilities, see David E. Sanger, Nicole Perlroth, and Julian E. Barnes, "As Understanding of Russian Hacking Grows, So Does Alarm," *New York Times*, January 2, 2021, http://nytimes.com/2021/01/02/us/politics/russian-hacking-government.html; David Ignatius, "Russia's SolarWinds Hack Was Espionage, Not an Act of War," *Washington Post*, December 22, 2020, http://washingtonpost.com/opinions/russias-solarwinds-hack-was-espionage-not-an-act-of-war/2020/12/22/ffa8f88a-4498-11eb-b0e4-0f182923a025_story.html.

198.   For similar views, see Newsham, "Taiwan War"; and Gompert, Cevallos, and Garafola, *War With China*, 56–57.

199.   For examples see "'War Will Benefit No One': Global Concern Over US-China Tensions," Al Jazeera, September 23, 2020, http://aljazeera.com/news/2020/9/23/war-will-benefit-no-one-world-concern-over-us-china-tensions; Jackson Diehl, "Trump Has Wasted His Chance to Rally U.S. Allies Against China," *Washington Post*, August 2, 2020, http://washingtonpost.com/opinions/global-opinions/trump-has-wasted-his-chance-to-rally-us-allies-against-china/2020/08/01/445c4750-d272-11ea-8c55-61e7fa5e82ab_story.html; and Shashank Bengali, "The U.S. Wants Asian Allies to Stand Up to China. It's Not That Easy," *Los Angeles Times*, July 14, 2020, http://latimes.com/world-nation/story/2020-07-14/the-u-s-wants-asian-allies-to-stand-up-to-china-heres-why-thats-hard.

ABOUT THE AUTHORS

Robert D. Blackwill is the Henry A. Kissinger senior fellow for U.S. foreign policy at the Council on Foreign Relations. He is also the Diller-von Furstenberg Family Foundation distinguished scholar at the Henry A. Kissinger Center for Global Affairs at Johns Hopkins University's School of Advanced International Studies. He is a former deputy assistant to the president, deputy national security advisor for strategic planning, and presidential envoy to Iraq under President George W. Bush. He was U.S. ambassador to India from 2001 to 2003. In 2016, he became the first U.S. ambassador to India since John Kenneth Galbraith to receive the Padma Bhushan Award from the government of India for distinguished service of a high order. Earlier in his career, he was the U.S. ambassador to conventional arms negotiations with the Warsaw Pact, director for European affairs at the National Security Council, principal deputy assistant secretary of state for political-military affairs, and principal deputy assistant secretary of state for European affairs. He is the author of the Council Special Reports *Revising U.S. Grand Strategy Toward China* (April 2015) coauthored with Ashley J. Tellis of the Carnegie Endowment for International Peace, *Xi Jinping on the Global Stage: Chinese Foreign Policy Under a Powerful but Exposed Leader* (February 2016) coauthored with Kurt M. Campbell of the Asia Group, and *Implementing Grand Strategy Toward China: Twenty-Two U.S. Policy Prescriptions* (January 2020).

Philip Zelikow is the White Burkett Miller professor of history and Wilson Newman professor of governance at the Miller Center, both at the University of Virginia. There he has also served as dean of the graduate school and director of the Miller Center of Public Affairs. His scholarly work, first at Harvard, later at Virginia, focuses on critical episodes in American and world history. Before and during his academic career, he has served at all levels of American government—federal, state, and local, including as an elected member of his town's school board. His full-time federal service began as a teacher for the U.S. Navy and then as a career foreign service officer, including work on the National Security Council staff for the elder President Bush. His last full-time government service was as counselor of the State Department, a deputy to Secretary of State Condoleezza Rice. In 2001, after the Florida problems, he directed the Carter-Ford commission on election reform that led to the Help America Vote Act of 2002. In 2003–04, he directed the 9/11 Commission. A former member of the President's Intelligence Advisory Board in two administrations (2001–03 and 2011–13), he was also a member of the Defense Policy Board (2015–17).